HAL LEONARD
GUITAR
TAB METHOD

Written by Jeff Schroedl

Contributing Editors: Jeff Arnold, Kurt Plahna, and Jim Schustedt

To access audio visit:
www.halleonard.com/mylibrary

"Enter Code"
5157-3282-6952-7649

ISBN 978-1-4584-3678-8

7777 W. BLUEMOUND RD. P.O. BOX 13819 MILWAUKEE, WI 53213

Visit Hal Leonard Online at
www.halleonard.com

CONTENTS

SONG INDEX

GETTING STARTED

PARTS OF THE GUITAR

This method is designed for use with an electric or acoustic guitar. Both are tuned the same, contain the same notes, and have mostly the same parts. The main difference is that acoustic guitars have a soundhole and are loud enough to be played without amplification, while electric guitars are plugged into an amp.

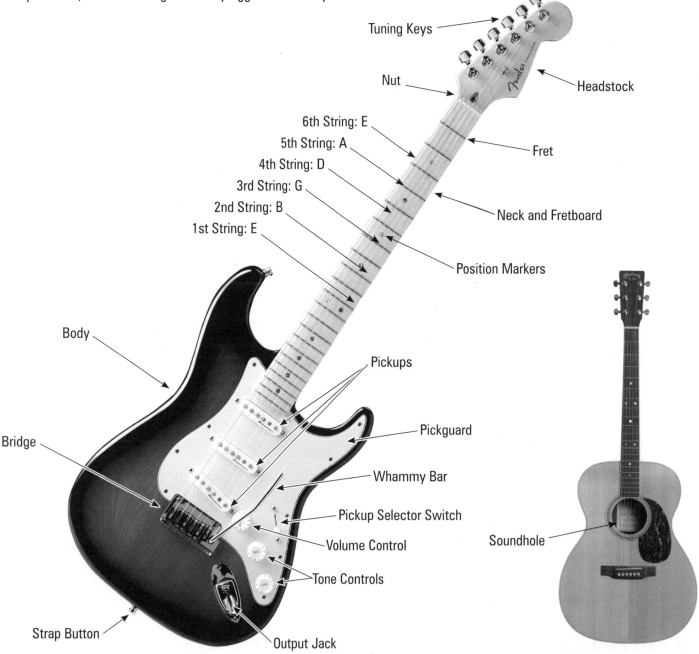

Tuning Keys

Nut

Headstock

6th String: E

5th String: A

4th String: D

3rd String: G

2nd String: B

1st String: E

Fret

Neck and Fretboard

Position Markers

Body

Pickups

Bridge

Pickguard

Whammy Bar

Pickup Selector Switch

Volume Control

Soundhole

Tone Controls

Strap Button

Output Jack

TUNING

The quickest and most accurate way to get in tune is to use an electronic tuner. You can either plug your guitar into the tuner or use the tuner's built-in microphone to tune an acoustic.

The guitar's six open strings should be tuned to these pitches:

E (thickest)–A–D–G–B–E (thinnest)

If you twist a string's tuning key clockwise, the pitch will become lower; if you twist the tuning key counterclockwise, the pitch will become higher.

Adjust the tuning keys until the electronic tuner's meter indicates that the pitch is correct. Or, listen to each string's correct pitch on the first audio track and slowly turn the tuning key until the sound of the string matches the sound on the track.

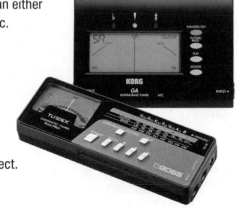

HOLDING THE GUITAR

Use the pictures below to help find a comfortable playing position. Whether you decide to sit or stand, it's important to remain relaxed and tension-free.

LEFT-HAND POSITION

Fingers are numbered 1 through 4. Arch your fingers and press the strings down firmly between the frets with your fingertips only.

Place your thumb on the underside of the guitar neck. Avoid letting the palm of your hand touch the neck of the guitar.

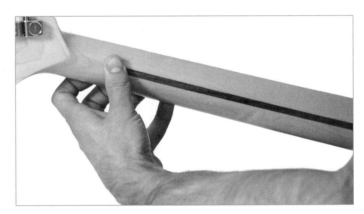

RIGHT-HAND POSITION

Hold the pick between your thumb and index finger. Strike the string with a downward motion approximately halfway between the bridge and neck.

The fingers not holding the pick may rest on the guitar for extra support.

THE LOW E STRING

Guitar music is written in a form of notation called **tablature**, or **tab** for short. Each line represents a string, and each number represents a fret. The thickest string played open, or not pressed, is the low E note. In tab, an open string is represented with a zero (0). The note F is located on the 1st fret. Press, or "fret" the string with your 1st finger, directly behind the first metal fret.

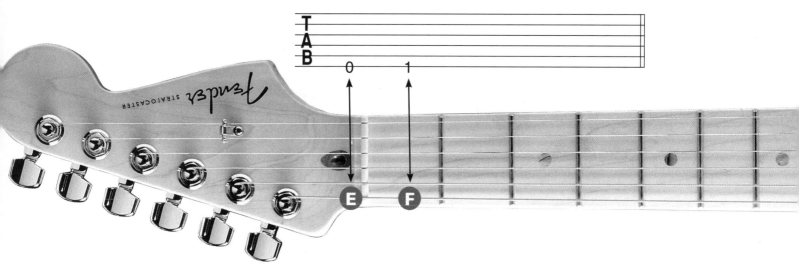

Play the theme from the movie *Jaws* using the notes E and F. Attack the string with a downstroke of the pick. Speed up as the numbers get closer together.

THEME FROM "JAWS" 🔊

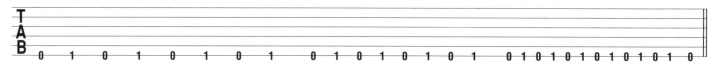

Now let's learn more notes on the low E string.

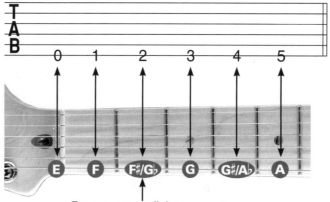

Two ways to spell the same note

GREEN ONIONS 🔊

"Green Onions" by Booker T. & the MG's uses the notes E, G, and A. Follow the tab and pick the notes at a steady speed, or **tempo**.

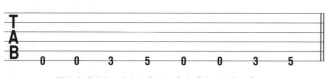

PETER GUNN 🔊

A **riff** is a short, composed phrase that is repeated. The popular riff from "Peter Gunn" is played with notes on the low E string.

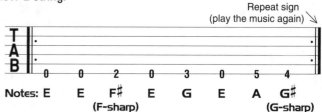

Notes: E   E   F♯   E   G   E   A   G♯
                    (F-sharp)   (G-sharp)

THE A STRING

Here are the notes within the first five frets of the 5th string, called the A string.

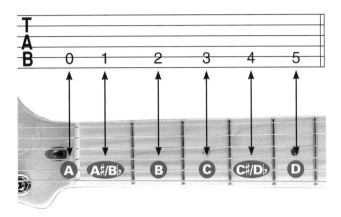

BRIT ROCK 🔊

This catchy riff uses the notes A, B, and C.

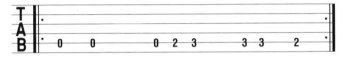

LEAN ON ME 🔊

This song was a #1 hit in two decades. It uses the notes A, B, C♯, and D.

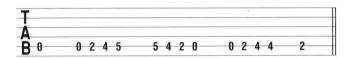

RHYTHM TAB

Rhythm tab adds rhythmic values to the basic tab staff. **Bar lines** divide music into **measures**. A **time signature** tells how many beats are in each measure and what kind of note is counted as one beat. In 4/4 time ("four-four"), there are four beats in each measure, and a **quarter note** is counted as one beat. It has a vertical stem joined to the tab number.

FEEL THE BEAT 🔊

Count "1, 2, 3, 4" as you play.

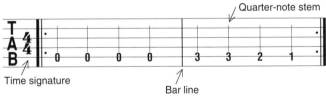

WORKING MAN 🔊

This classic riff by the band Rush uses quarter notes on strings 5 and 6.

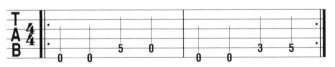

ZEPPELIN TRIBUTE 🔊

Anchor the palm of your pick hand on the bridge of the guitar to help your picking accuracy.

BLUES RIFF 🔊

Use the 3rd finger of your fret hand for notes on the 4th fret, 1st finger for the note on the 2nd fret, and 4th finger (pinky) for the note on the 5th fret.

MORE RIFFS

The next two riffs are written in **3/4 time**. This means there are three beats in each measure, and a quarter note receives one beat.

MY NAME IS JONAS

Count "1–2–3, 1–2–3" as you play this riff by the band Weezer.

Words and Music by Rivers Cuomo, Patrick Wilson and Jason Cropper
Copyright © 1994 E.O. Smith Music, Fie! and Ubermommasuprapoppa Music
All Rights for E.O. Smith Music and Fie! Administered by Wixen Music Publishing, Inc.

MALAGUEÑA

This traditional Spanish piece is very popular among classical guitarists.

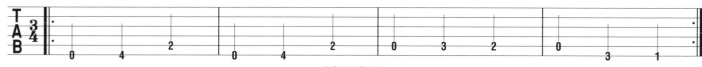

By Francisco Tarrega
Copyright © 2012 by HAL LEONARD CORPORATION

A **half note** lasts two beats. It fills the time of two quarter notes. In tab, a circle surrounds the tab number(s) and is attached to a vertical stem.

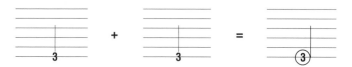

CANON IN D

The first line is played with half notes and the second line is played with quarter notes. Count aloud and keep a steady tempo.

Count: one two three four etc.

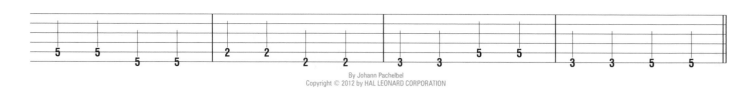

By Johann Pachelbel
Copyright © 2012 by HAL LEONARD CORPORATION

ELECTRIC FUNERAL

The heavy metal band Black Sabbath used half notes and quarter notes for this powerful, eerie riff.

Words and Music by Frank Iommi, John Osbourne, William Ward and Terence Butler
© Copyright 1970 (Renewed) and 1974 (Renewed) Onward Music Ltd., London, England
TRO - Essex Music International, Inc., New York, controls all publication rights for the U.S.A. and Canada

COOL GROOVE

Now try playing half notes in 3/4 time.

Copyright © 2012 by HAL LEONARD CORPORATION

An **eighth note** lasts half a beat, or half as long as a quarter note. One eighth note is written with a stem and flag; consecutive eighth notes are connected with a beam.

LADY MADONNA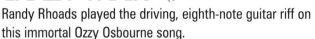

While playing this Beatles classic, count with the word "and" between the beats.

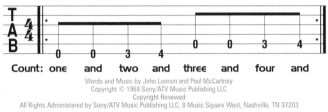

Count: one and two and three and four and

CRAZY TRAIN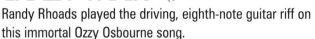

Randy Rhoads played the driving, eighth-note guitar riff on this immortal Ozzy Osbourne song.

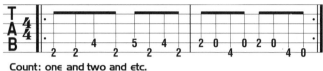

Count: one and two and etc.

AQUALUNG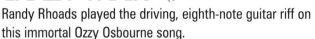

Now let's mix eighth notes and quarter notes on this famous Jethro Tull song.

GREEN-EYED LADY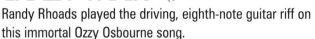

Experiment to determine which fingers work best for this classic Sugarloaf riff. Just be sure to use your fingertips; don't play "flat-fingered."

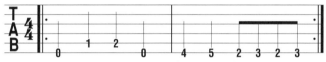

A **rest** is a symbol used to indicate silence in music. In 4/4 time, a **quarter rest** fills the time of one beat and a **half rest** fills the time of two beats.

Quarter Rest
One Beat

Half Rest
Two Beats

25 OR 6 TO 4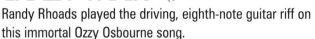

This riff by the band Chicago uses a quarter rest. Mute the string by touching it gently with the palm of your picking hand. You can also release the pressure of your fret hand to silence the string.

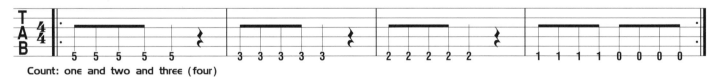

Count: one and two and three (four)

BRAIN STEW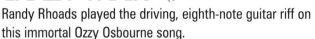

The band Green Day used a similar descending pattern for this hit song, which uses quarter and half rests.

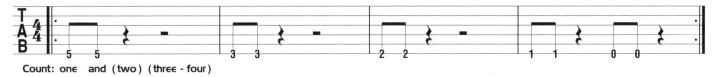

Count: one and (two) (three - four)

THE D STRING

Here are the notes within the first five frets of the 4th string, called the D string.

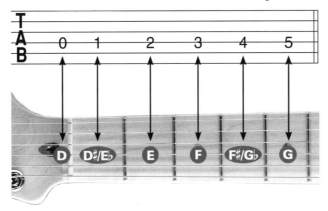

D-MENTED

Say the note names aloud as you play this sinister riff.

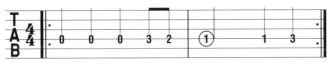

MACHINE GUN

Jimi Hendrix used this riff as the foundation for his song from the album *Band of Gypsys*. The dot below beat 3 is called a **staccato** mark. It tells you to cut the note short.

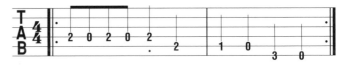

OH, PRETTY WOMAN

This Roy Orbison song features one of the most recognizable riffs of all time.

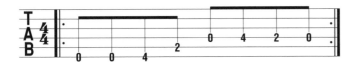

YOU GIVE LOVE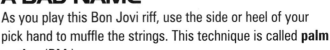
A BAD NAME

As you play this Bon Jovi riff, use the side or heel of your pick hand to muffle the strings. This technique is called **palm muting** (P.M.).

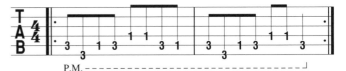

A **tie** is a curved, dashed line connecting two notes of the same pitch. It tells you not to strike the second note. The first note should be struck and held for the combined value of both notes.

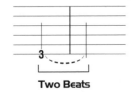

Two Beats

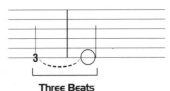

Three Beats

One Beat

SPACE TRUCKIN'

You're now ready to tackle this driving riff from the band Deep Purple.

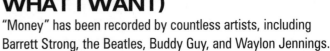

MONEY (THAT'S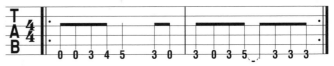
WHAT I WANT)

"Money" has been recorded by countless artists, including Barrett Strong, the Beatles, Buddy Guy, and Waylon Jennings.

An **eighth rest** indicates to be silent for half a beat. It looks like this: 𝄾

HAVA NAGILA
Start slowly and use your pinky for the G♯ on the 4th fret.

Count: one two (three) and four and

SUPER FREAK
This funky Rick James hit uses both eighth and quarter rests.

JAMIE'S CRYIN'
This Van Halen riff uses both eighth rests and ties.

DAY TRIPPER
On this Beatles classic, you'll get a workout on all three bottom strings.

The next riffs begin with **pickup notes**. Count pickup notes as if they were the last portion of a full measure.

YOU REALLY GOT ME
Van Halen covered this Kinks song on their first album.

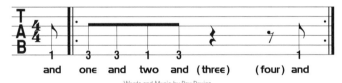

and one and two and (three) (four) and

COME AS YOU ARE
This Nirvana riff begins on the "and" of beat 3.

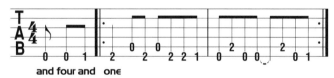

and four and one

MISSISSIPPI QUEEN
A wavy line over a note indicates to apply **vibrato**, a technique produced by pulling (bending) and releasing a string in rapid succession.

FEEL YOUR LOVE TONIGHT
Here's another Van Halen riff. This one applies palm muting and vibrato.

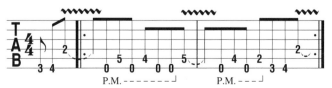

P.M. ---------┘   P.M. ---┘

WIPE OUT

Now it's time to play your first complete song. "Wipe Out" is one of the most popular instrumental hits of all time. It was originally recorded by the Surfaris in 1963 and has been performed since by numerous groups, including the Ventures and the Beach Boys.

During the famous drum breakdown in the second half of the song, you'll notice a **whole rest**. It indicates one full measure of silence, and looks like this:

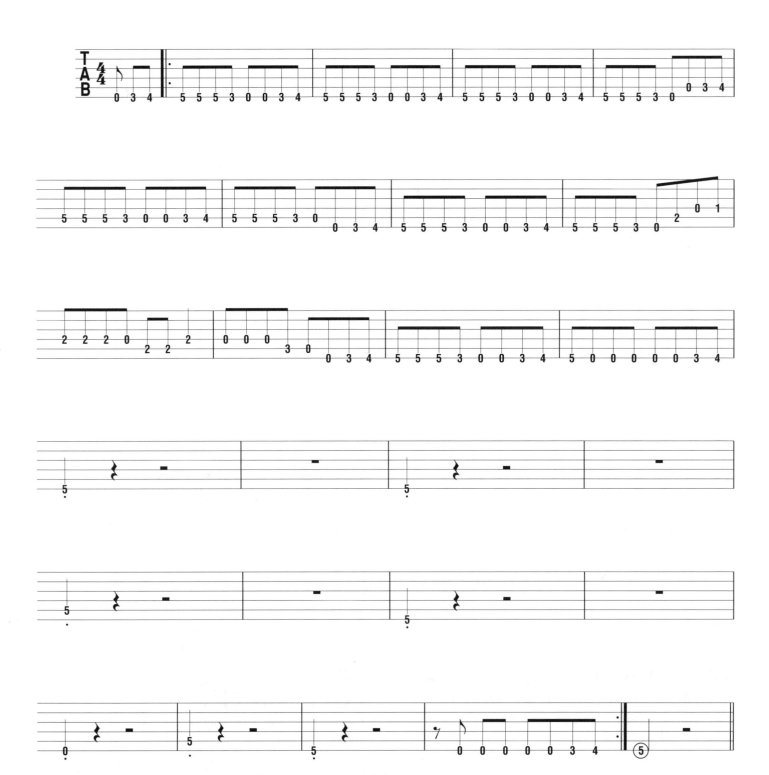

POWER CHORDS

A **power chord** consists of two notes played together. Rock guitarists use power chords to create a low, powerful sound.

The lower note of a power chord is called the **root note**. It is the note upon which the chord is named. The power chord label also includes the suffix "5."

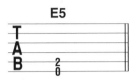

METALLIC

Attack both notes of the power chord at the same time with a single downstroke.

JACK HAMMER

Remember to stop the chords from ringing when you see rests or staccato dots.

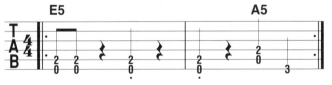

T.N.T.

Australian hard rock band AC/DC uses power chords in many songs, including this classic riff from "T.N.T."

Words and Music by Angus Young, Malcolm Young and Bon Scott

MOVABLE POWER CHORDS

Power chords can be played up and down the lower strings of the guitar fretboard using one simple fingering shape. Use your 1st and 3rd fingers as shown below.

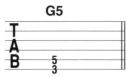

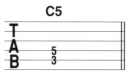

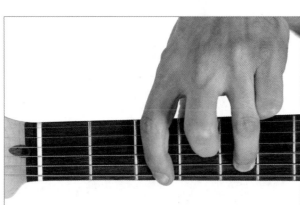

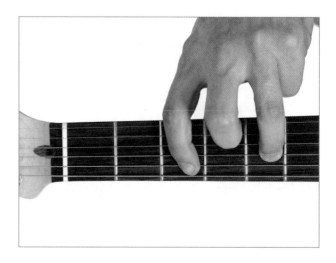

A power chord's name comes from its root note, or where your 1st finger is placed on the fretboard. Here is a diagram of the notes you've learned so far within the first five frets of strings 5 and 6, and the power chords built upon these roots.

ROOT ON 6TH STRING

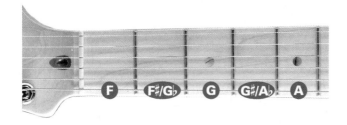

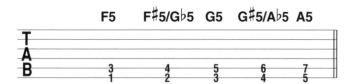

ROOT ON 5TH STRING

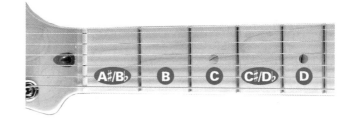

ALL ALONG THE 🔊 WATCHTOWER

Bob Dylan, Jimi Hendrix, and others have recorded this song. The root note of all three power chords is on the 6th string.

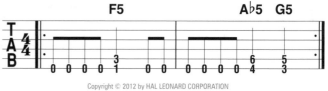

MEGA-HEAVY 🔊

This riff chugs on the low E string between power chord attacks.

SMELLS LIKE TEEN SPIRIT

This Nirvana hit uses power chords with roots on the 5th and 6th strings.

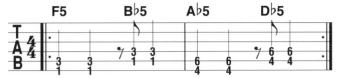

I CAN'T EXPLAIN

Guitarist Pete Townshend of the Who used power chords in many songs, including "I Can't Explain."

When a **dot** appears after a note, you extend the note by half its value. A **dotted half note** lasts for three beats.

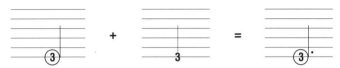

A **whole note** is twice as long as a half note; it lasts four beats. A whole note is written in a circle with no stem.

BABA O'RILEY

Now let's mix movable and open power chords to play another rock classic by the Who.

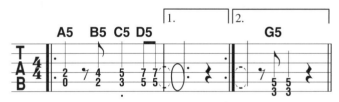

OWNER OF A LONELY HEART

This riff by the band Yes is tabbed with **ending brackets**. The 1st time through, play the 1st ending and repeat as usual. The 2nd time, skip the 1st ending and play the 2nd ending.

JAILBREAK

Power chords are often mixed with single notes. Try this riff popularized by the band Thin Lizzy.

REFUGEE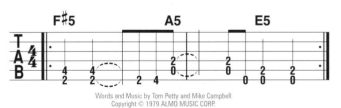

Tom Petty's "Refugee" also puts power chords and single notes to good use.

BATMAN THEME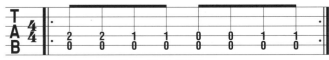

Here's an easy, fun riff that is a variation of the open A5 power chord.

CHICAGO BLUES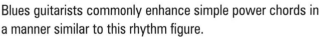

Blues guitarists commonly enhance simple power chords in a manner similar to this rhythm figure.

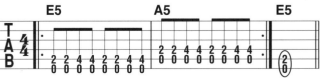

WILD THING

"Wild Thing" is one of rock music's most enduring songs. Originally a #1 hit for the Troggs in 1966, it has since been recorded by Jimi Hendrix, Sam Kinison, and many others. The entire song can be played using movable power chords.

Intro

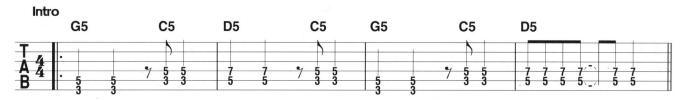

Chorus

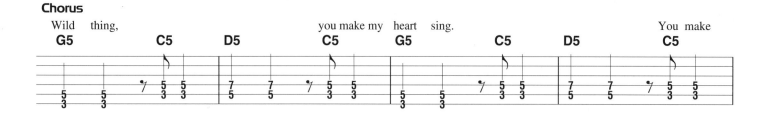

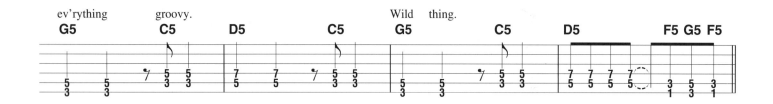

Verse

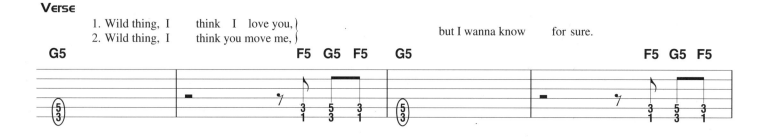

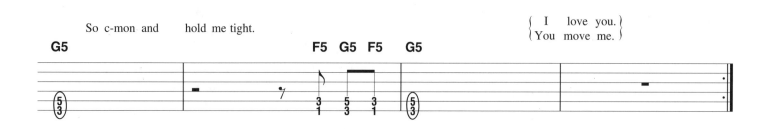

Outro-Chorus

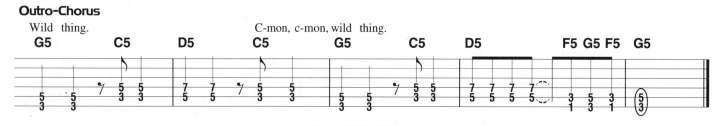

Words and Music by Chip Taylor
© 1965 (Renewed 1993) EMI BLACKWOOD MUSIC INC.

CHECKPOINT

You're halfway through Book One and well on your way to a rewarding hobby or a successful career with the guitar. Let's take a moment to review some of what you've learned so far.

NOTE NAMES

Draw a line to match each note on the left with its correct name on the right.

C

B

G

E

F

A

D

SYMBOLS & TERMS

Draw a line to match each symbol on the left with its correct name on the right.

Palm Mute

Half Note

Eighth Rest

Quarter Rest

Eighth Note

Repeat Sign

Power Chord

Write the note names in the spaces provided.

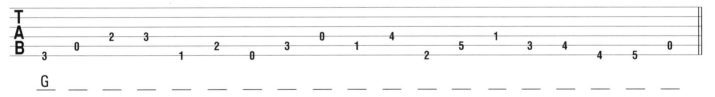

G

Add bar lines.

Below the tab staff are note names. Write the notes on the tab staff.

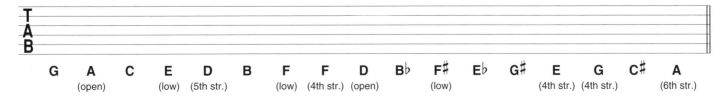

G	A	C	E	D	B	F	F	D	B♭	F♯	E♭	G♯	E	G	C♯	A
(open)		(low)	(5th str.)		(low)		(4th str.)	(open)		(low)			(4th str.)	(4th str.)		(6th str.)

THE G STRING

Here are the notes within the first five frets of the 3rd string, called the G string.

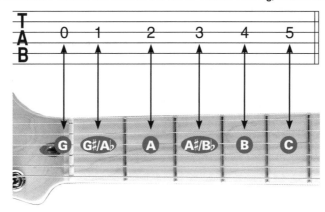

NORWEGIAN WOOD (THIS BIRD HAS FLOWN)

This Indian-influenced Beatles song, written in 3/4 time, was the first rock song to feature a sitar on a recording.

DON'T FEAR THE REAPER

In some songs, like this cowbell-infused classic by Blue Öyster Cult, it's common to see the instruction **"let ring."** Instead of releasing your fingers after each note is played, you hold them down, allowing the notes to sustain.

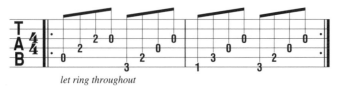

let ring throughout

LA BAMBA

This song has been recorded by Ritchie Valens, Los Lobos, and many others. It uses notes on all four strings you've learned so far. Use your 2nd finger to press the notes on the 2nd fret and 3rd finger on the 3rd fret.

SMOKE ON THE WATER

Deep Purple's "Smoke on the Water" features one of the greatest rock riffs of all time. Strike the two-note chords, or **dyads**, with downstrokes. Although you haven't learned notes beyond the 5th fret, simply use your 3rd finger to press the notes on the 6th fret.

PIPELINE

"Pipeline" is a classic guitar instrumental. The original version was a surf-rock hit for the Chantays in 1963, and it has since been recorded by the Ventures, Dick Dale, Stevie Ray Vaughan, and others. It uses single notes on the bottom four strings, as well as a few power chords. In the A section, fret the B note (5th string, 2nd fret) for the entire four measures.

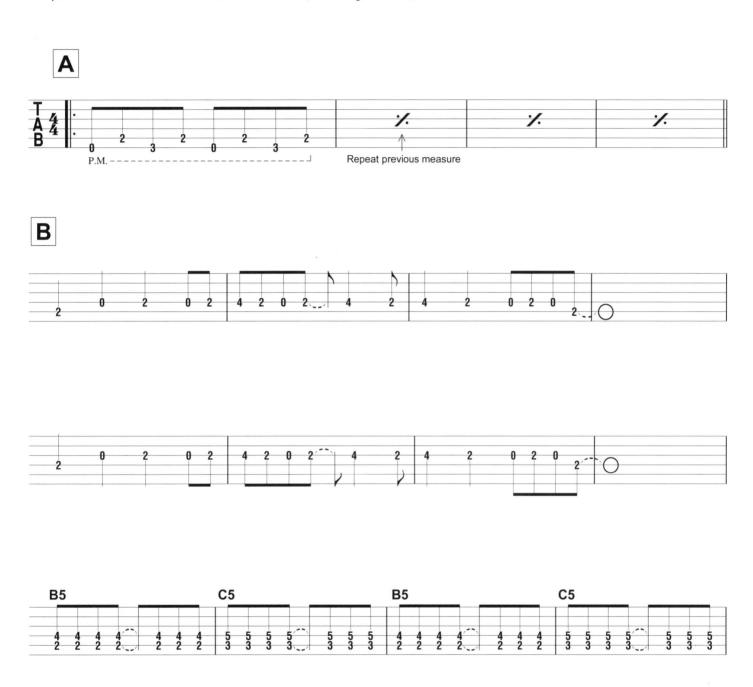

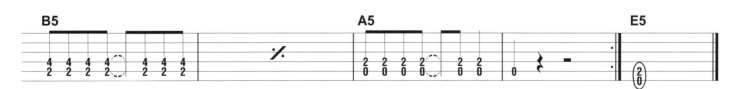

By Bob Spickard and Brian Carman
Copyright © 1962, 1963 (Renewed) by Regent Music Corporation (BMI)

THE B STRING

Here are the notes within the first five frets of the 2nd string, called the B string.

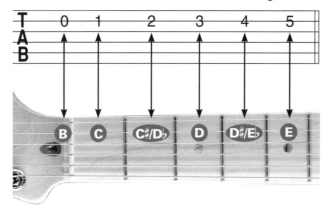

DUELIN' BANJOS

This bluegrass theme was featured in the movie *Deliverance.*

SUSIE-Q

Creedence Clearwater Revival covered this Dale Hawkins song on their first album.

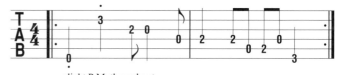

slight P.M. throughout

FÜR ELISE

This instantly recognizable piece in 3/4 time is truly a classic. Beethoven wrote it in 1810.

WALK DON'T RUN

The Ventures, Chet Atkins, and others have recorded this popular instrumental song.

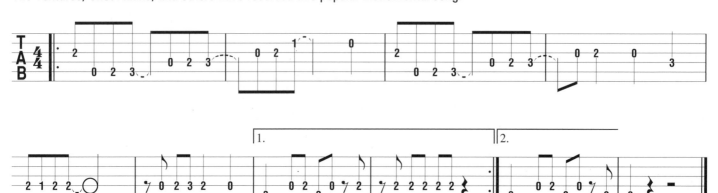

THE HIGH E STRING

Here are the notes within the first five frets of the 1st string, called the E string.

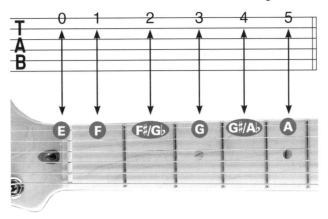

IN MY LIFE

The opening riff of this song by the Beatles uses notes on the top two strings. Fret-hand fingerings are indicated below the tab staff.

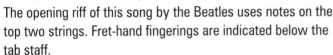

Fret-hand fingers: 1   4   1   2   0   3

Words and Music by John Lennon and Paul McCartney
Copyright © 1965 Sony/ATV Music Publishing LLC
Copyright Renewed
All Rights Administered by Sony/ATV Music Publishing LLC, 8 Music Square West, Nashville, TN 37203

TICKET TO RIDE

Here's another classic intro by the Beatles. Keep your 1st finger planted on the first note and let the strings ring throughout.

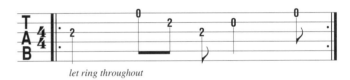

let ring throughout

Words and Music by John Lennon and Paul McCartney
Copyright © 1965 Sony/ATV Music Publishing LLC
Copyright Renewed
All Rights Administered by Sony/ATV Music Publishing LLC, 8 Music Square West, Nashville, TN 37203

REBEL, REBEL

To play this David Bowie riff, follow the "let ring" indications and be sure to mute the low E note in the 2nd measure with your palm.

let ring - - - - - - - - - - ┘   P.M. *let ring - - - - ┘*

Words and Music by David Bowie
© 1974 (Renewed 2002) EMI MUSIC PUBLISHING LTD., JONES MUSIC AMERICA and CHRYSALIS MUSIC
All Rights for EMI MUSIC PUBLISHING LTD. Controlled and Administered by COLGEMS-EMI MUSIC INC.
All Rights for JONES MUSIC AMERICA Administered by ARZO PUBLISHING
All Rights for CHRYSALIS MUSIC Administered by BMG RIGHTS MANAGEMENT (US) LLC

SUNDAY BLOODY SUNDAY

Now play this riff by the band U2, paying close attention to the fingerings below the tab. Keep the notes depressed so they ring, and lay your 1st finger across the top three strings at the 2nd fret for the last half of measure 1.

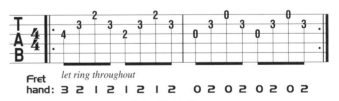

let ring throughout

Fret hand: 3   2   1   2   1   2   1   2   0   2   0   2   0   2   0   2

Words and Music by U2
Copyright © 1983 UNIVERSAL MUSIC PUBLISHING INTERNATIONAL B.V.
All Rights in the United States and Canada Controlled and Administered by
UNIVERSAL - POLYGRAM INTERNATIONAL PUBLISHING, INC.

FOXEY LADY

Here is one of Jimi Hendrix's signature riffs. Lay your pinky across the top two strings to play the notes at the 5th fret.

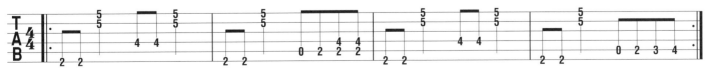

Words and Music by Jimi Hendrix
Copyright © 1967, 1968, 1980 by EXPERIENCE HENDRIX, L.L.C.
Copyright Renewed 1995, 1996
All Rights Controlled and Administered by EXPERIENCE HENDRIX, L.L.C.

JAMES BOND THEME

DEMO   MINUS GTR. 1   MINUS GTR. 2

The main theme of the James Bond films is powerful, mysterious, and instantly recognizable. It contains notes on all six strings, and is arranged here as a duet for two guitars. Pick a part and play!

Once you've reached the end of section E, you'll see the instructions "D.S. al Coda (no repeat)." Jump back to the sign (𝄋) at letter B and play up to the instruction "To Coda." At this point, jump to the last line of the tune where it's labeled "Coda," and play the final five measures.

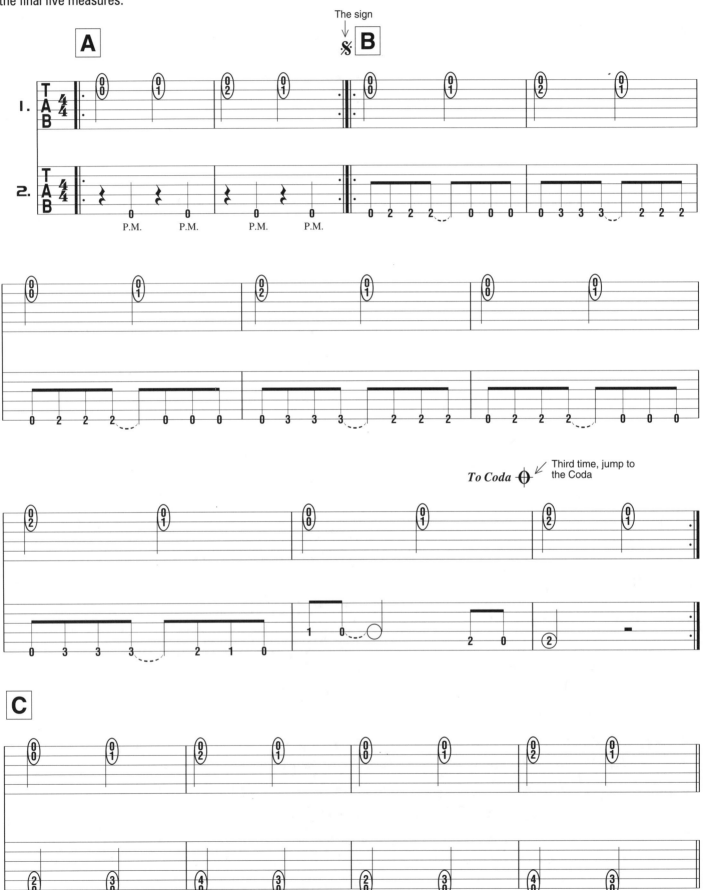

OPEN CHORDS

Chords that contain open strings are called open-position chords, or simply **open chords**. They are used for accompaniment, or **rhythm guitar**, and usually incorporate four, five, or all six strings.

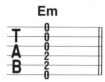

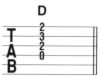

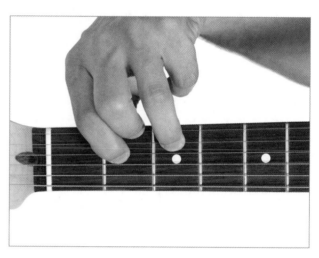

GET UP STAND UP

Playing chords in a rhythmic pattern is called **strumming**. Strum the E minor chord in a downward motion to play a basic version of this Bob Marley song.

1. Get up,   stand up.   Stand up   for   your right.
2. Get up,   stand up.   Don't   give up   the fight.

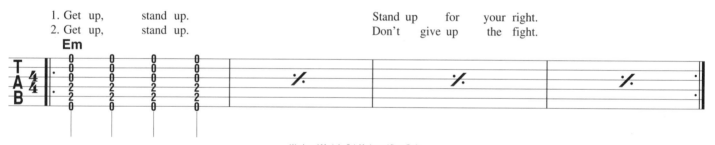

Words and Music by Bob Marley and Peter Tosh
Copyright © 1974 Fifty-Six Hope Road Music Ltd., Odnil Music Ltd., State One Music America LLC and Embassy Music Corporation
Copyright Renewed
All Rights in North America Administered by Blue Mountain Music Ltd./Irish Town Songs (ASCAP) and throughout the rest of the world by Blue Mountain Music Ltd. (PRS)

LAND OF A THOUSAND DANCES

Now try the D chord for this Wilson Pickett classic. Arch your fingers and play on the tips to avoid touching the other strings.

Na,   na, na, na, na,   na, na, na, na,   na, na, na,   na, na, na.

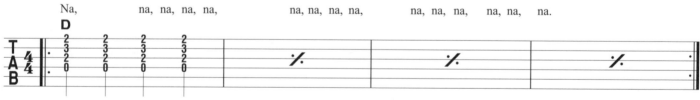

Words and Music by Chris Kenner
© 1963, 1970 (Renewed 1991) EMI LONGITUDE MUSIC

HEART OF GOLD

Let's practice changing between two chords with the intro from one of Neil Young's greatest hits.

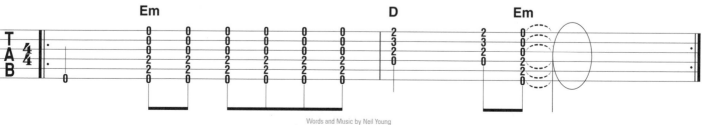

Words and Music by Neil Young
Copyright © 1971 by Silver Fiddle Music
Copyright Renewed

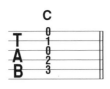
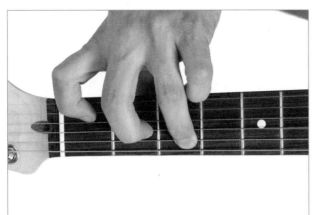
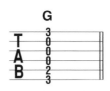
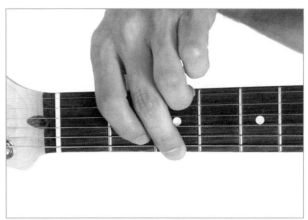

YELLOW SUBMARINE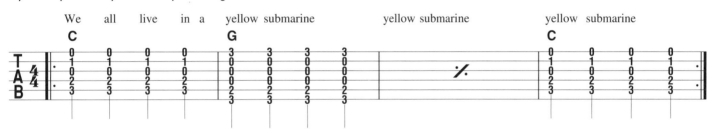

Try to keep a steady strum as you change chords for this all-time Beatles favorite.

SPACE ODDITY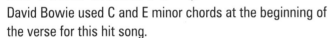

David Bowie used C and E minor chords at the beginning of the verse for this hit song.

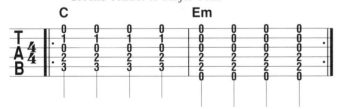

SHOULD I STAY OR SHOULD I GO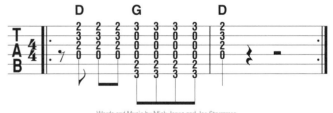

Open D and G chords kick off the intro of this classic by the Clash.

WONDERFUL TONIGHT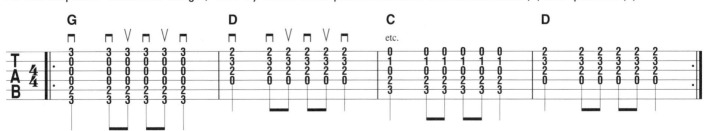

For Eric Clapton's "Wonderful Tonight," let's try a new strum pattern that uses both downstrokes ( ) and upstrokes ( ).

WILD NIGHT

Van Morrison's "Wild Night" is a certified rock classic and has been covered by numerous artists. It uses all four open chords introduced so far. Play the strum patterns written or feel free to try your own variations.

Intro

1. As you brush your

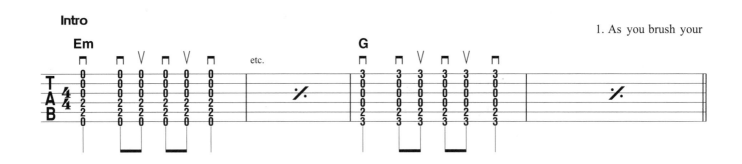

Verse

shoes,   and stand before   the mirror   and you comb
girls walk by,   dressed up for   each other   and the boys

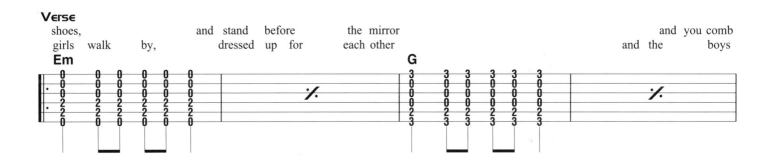

your hair,   and grab your coat and hat.   And you walk
do the boogie woogie   on the corner of the street.   And the

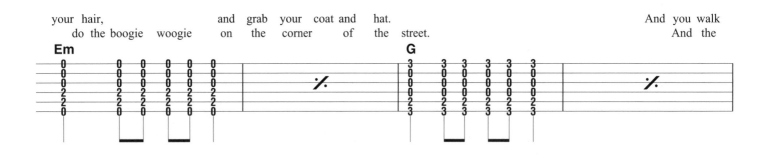

wet streets try - in' to re - mem - ber   all the wild
people passin' by   just stare in wild wonder   and the

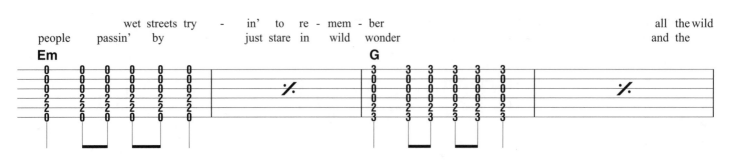

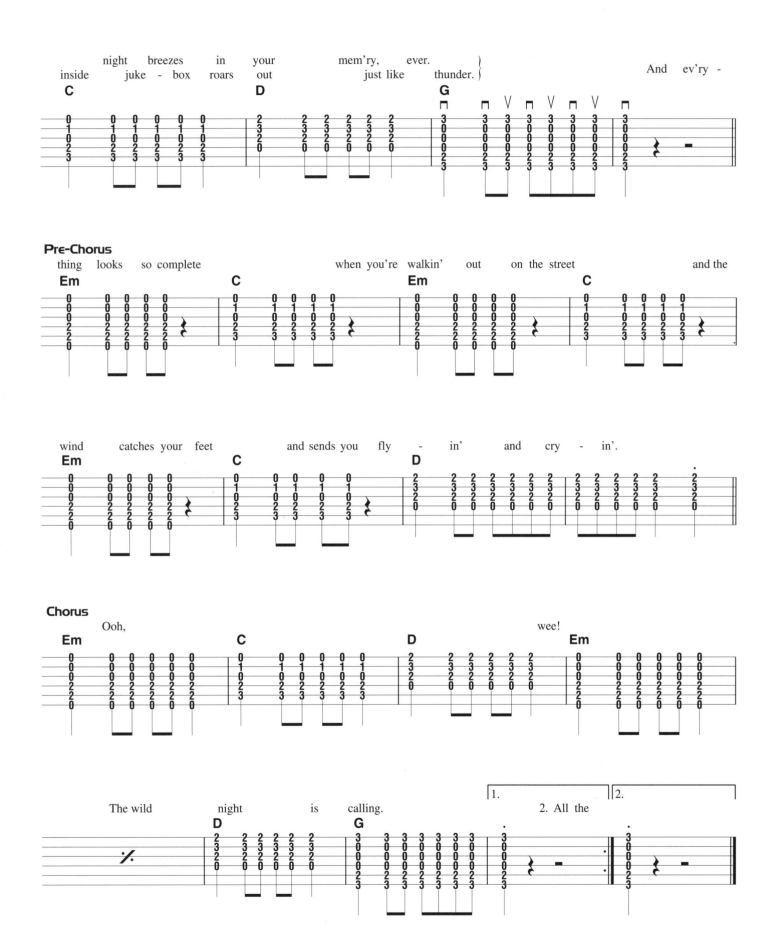

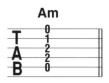

Am

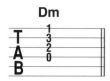

Dm

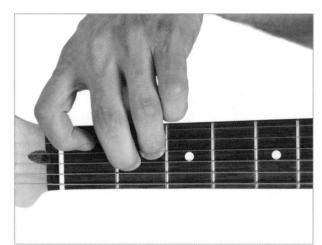

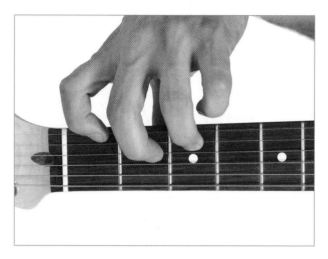

EVIL WAYS

Let's give your new A minor chord a workout with one of Santana's greatest hits. Listen to the audio to help you with the rhythms. Use the palm of your pick hand to silence the strings during the rests.

LOUIE, LOUIE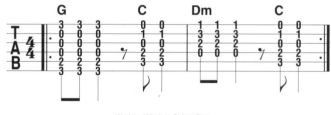

"Louie, Louie" is a rock 'n' roll standard and has been recorded by hundreds of artists. Its three-chord riff is instantly recognizable.

AIN'T NO SUNSHINE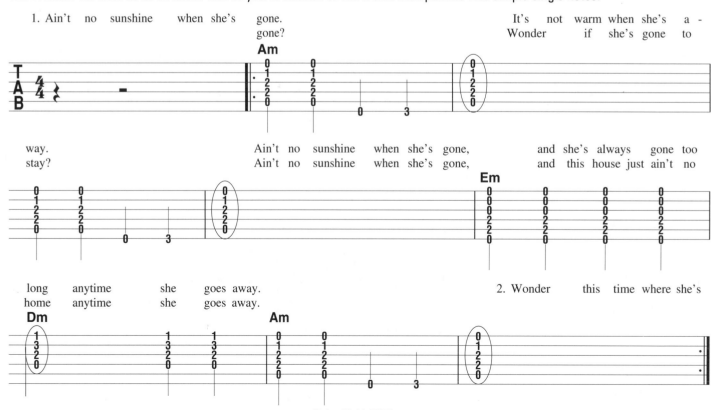

Bill Withers' hit uses all three minor chords you've learned so far. It also incorporates two simple single notes.

KNOCKIN' ON HEAVEN'S DOOR

Bob Dylan's timeless ballad uses open chords exclusively. Follow the strumming rhythms notated or just read the chord symbols and improvise your own strum patterns.

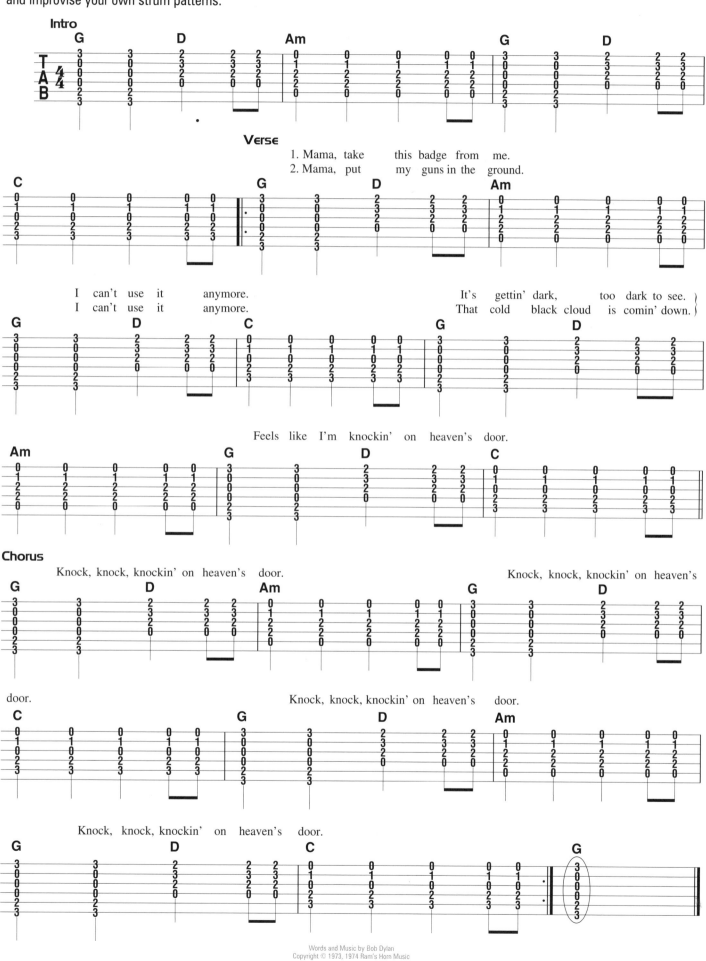

Words and Music by Bob Dylan
Copyright © 1973, 1974 Ram's Horn Music

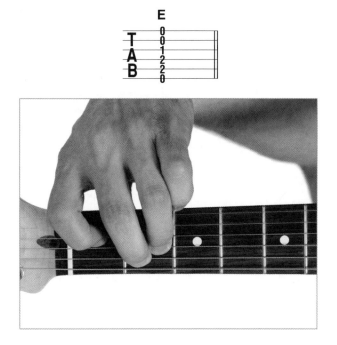

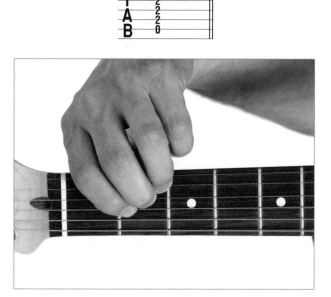

ABOUT A GIRL

For songs that change chords quickly, like this one by Nirvana, it's okay to release your fingers from one chord early in order to arrive at the next chord on time. It's natural for a few open strings to be struck in the transition.

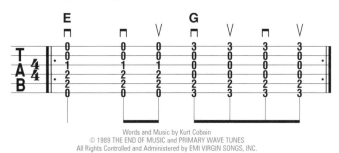

Words and Music by Kurt Cobain
© 1989 THE END OF MUSIC and PRIMARY WAVE TUNES
All Rights Controlled and Administered by EMI VIRGIN SONGS, INC.

R.O.C.K. IN THE U.S.A.

When using up/down strumming, don't worry about hitting every single string on the upstroke. It's okay to just play three or four notes of the chords, or whatever feels natural.

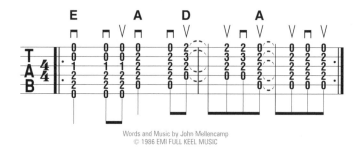

Words and Music by John Mellencamp
© 1986 EMI FULL KEEL MUSIC

BYE BYE LOVE

Another way to play an A chord is to lay your 1st finger across the top four strings at the 2nd fret. Many rock guitarists use this fingering and simply mute or miss the high E string. Experiment and choose which version works best for you in this hit by the Everly Brothers.

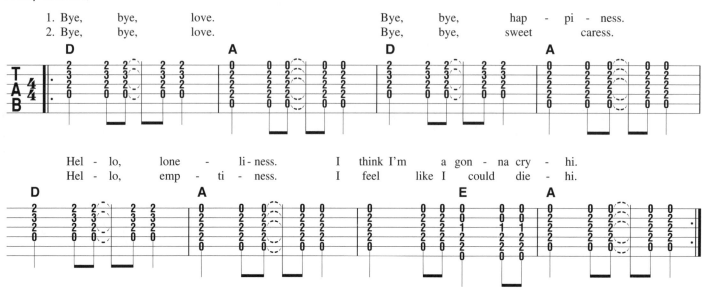

1. Bye, bye, love. Bye, bye, hap - pi - ness.
2. Bye, bye, love. Bye, bye, sweet caress.

Hel - lo, lone - li - ness. I think I'm a gon - na cry - hi.
Hel - lo, emp - ti - ness. I feel like I could die - hi.

Words and Music by Felice Bryant and Boudleaux Bryant
Copyright © 1957 by HOUSE OF BRYANT PUBLICATIONS, Gatlinburg, TN
Copyright Renewed
All Foreign Rights Controlled by SONY/ATV MUSIC PUBLISHING LLC
All Rights for SONY/ATV MUSIC PUBLISHING LLC Administered by SONY/ATV MUSIC PUBLISHING LLC, 8 Music Square West, Nashville, TN 37203

PATIENCE

Here's a hit song by Guns N' Roses that uses five open chords.

Verse

1. Shed a tear 'cause I'm missin' you,   I'm still alright to smile.
2. Was a time when I wasn't sure but you   set my mind at ease.

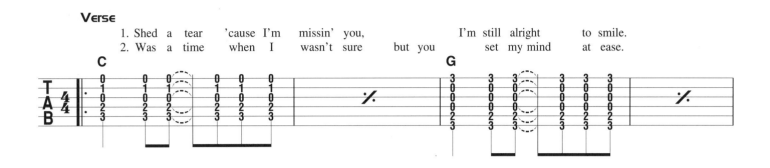

Girl, I think about you ev - 'ry day now.
There is no doubt you're in my heart now.

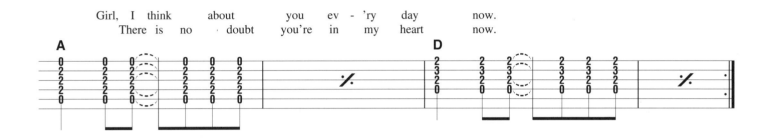

Chorus

Said, woman, take it slow, it'll work itself out fine.
Said, sugar, make it slow, and we come togeth - er fine.

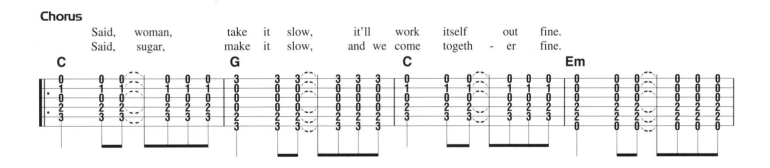

All we need is just a lit - tle pa - tience.
All we need is just a lit - tle pa - tience.

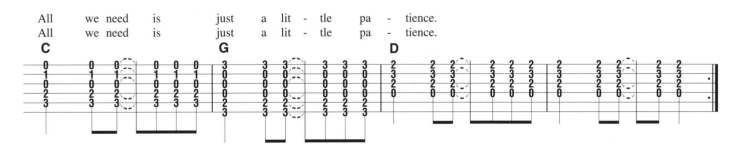

SLIDES, HAMMER-ONS & PULL-OFFS

Sometimes, it's not so much what you play, it's how you play it. In music terms, this is called **articulation**. Slides, hammer-ons, and pull-offs all belong to a special category of articulations called **legato**. Legato techniques allow you to connect two or more consecutive notes together to create a smooth, flowing sound.

To play a **slide**, pick the first note as you normally would. Then, maintain pressure as you move your fret-hand finger up or down the fretboard to sound the second note. (The second note is not picked.) In tab, a slide is indicated with a short, slanted line and a curved **slur**.

MY SHARONA

Use your 1st finger to do the sliding for this riff by the Knack.

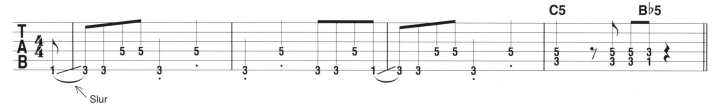

Words and Music by Doug Fieger and Berton Averre
Copyright © 1979 by Three Wise Boys Music, LLC (BMI), Small Hill Music (ASCAP) and Eighties Music (ASCAP)
All Rights for Small Hill Music and Eighties Music Controlled and Administered by Hi Pitch Music Services

BOOM BOOM

Now try this John Lee Hooker blues riff. The slide is played with the 3rd finger. This allows your 2nd finger to play the notes on the 3rd fret and your 1st finger to play the notes on the 2nd fret.

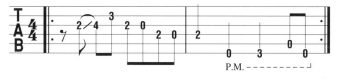

Words and Music by John Lee Hooker
Copyright © 1962 (Renewed) by Conrad Music
All Rights Administered by BMG Chrysalis

SWEET LEAF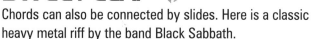

Chords can also be connected by slides. Here is a classic heavy metal riff by the band Black Sabbath.

Words and Music by Frank Iommi, John Osbourne, William Ward and Terence Butler
© Copyright 1971 (Renewed) and 1974 (Renewed) Westminster Music Ltd., London, England
TRO - Essex Music International, Inc., New York, controls all publication rights for the U.S.A. and Canada

To play a **hammer-on**, pick the first note and then press down, or "hammer on" to, a higher note along the same string. The initial attack should carry the tone over both notes.

LIFE IN THE FAST LANE

Here's a famous guitar intro by the Eagles. Use your 1st finger to play the notes on the 2nd fret.

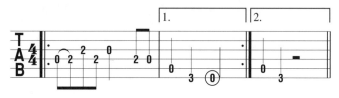

Words and Music by Don Henley, Glenn Frey and Joe Walsh
© 1976 (Renewed) CASS COUNTY MUSIC, RED CLOUD MUSIC and WOW & FLUTTER MUSIC

PAPERBACK WRITER

For this Beatles riff, lay your 1st finger across the bottom three strings at the 3rd fret. Maintain pressure as you use your 3rd and 4th fingers to play the notes on the 5th fret.

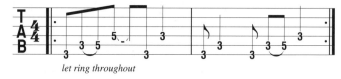

let ring throughout

Words and Music by John Lennon and Paul McCartney
Copyright © 1966 Sony/ATV Music Publishing LLC
Copyright Renewed
All Rights Administered by Sony/ATV Music Publishing LLC, 8 Music Square West, Nashville, TN 37203

A **pull-off** is the opposite of a hammer-on. First, start with both fingers planted. Pick the higher note, then tug or "pull" that finger off the string to sound the lower note, which is already fretted by the lower finger.

BRING IT ON HOME

This riff by Led Zeppelin features pull-offs on the 3rd string.

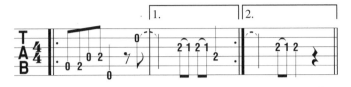

Written by Willie Dixon
© 1964 (Renewed 1992) HOOCHIE COOCHIE MUSIC (BMI)/Administered by BUG MUSIC

CULT OF PERSONALITY

Notes can also be pulled off to open strings, as this riff by Living Colour demonstrates.

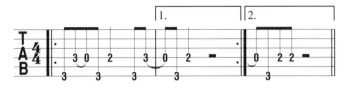

Words and Music by William Calhoun, Corey Glover, Muzz Skillings and Vernon Reid
Copyright © 1988 Sony/ATV Music Publishing LLC, Dare To Dream Music, Darkology Music,
Teenage Dog Music and Muzz Skillings Designee
All Rights Administered by Sony/ATV Music Publishing LLC, 8 Music Square West, Nashville, TN 37203

Of course, slides, hammer-ons, and pull-offs can be used in any combination. Here are a few examples.

THE MAN WHO SOLD THE WORLD

This David Bowie song was famously covered by Nirvana on MTV's *Unplugged*. For the back-to-back hammer-pull in the 2nd measure, only the first of the three notes is picked.

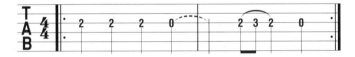

Words and Music by David Bowie
© 1971 (Renewed 1999) EMI MUSIC PUBLISHING LTD., TINTORETTO MUSIC and CHRYSALIS MUSIC
All Rights for EMI MUSIC PUBLISHING LTD. Controlled and Administered by SCREEN GEMS-EMI MUSIC INC.
All Rights for TINTORETTO MUSIC Administered by RZO MUSIC
All Rights for CHRYSALIS MUSIC Administered by BMG RIGHTS MANAGEMENT (US) LLC

COME OUT AND PLAY

The Offspring's "Come Out and Play" contains hammer-ons and slides. The first part of the slide occurs very quickly and is called a **grace-note slide**.

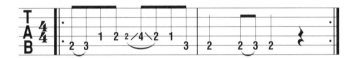

Words and Music by Dexter Holland
Copyright © 1994 Gamete Music (BMI)

BLUEGRASS RUN

Legato articulations are common in all styles of guitar music. Here's a fun bluegrass lick that uses all three types of slurs introduced so far.

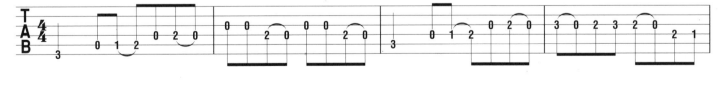

HEY JOE

What better way to wrap up Book One than with one of Jimi Hendrix's biggest hits. "Hey Joe" contains several chords, single notes on all six strings, slides, hammer-ons, and more!

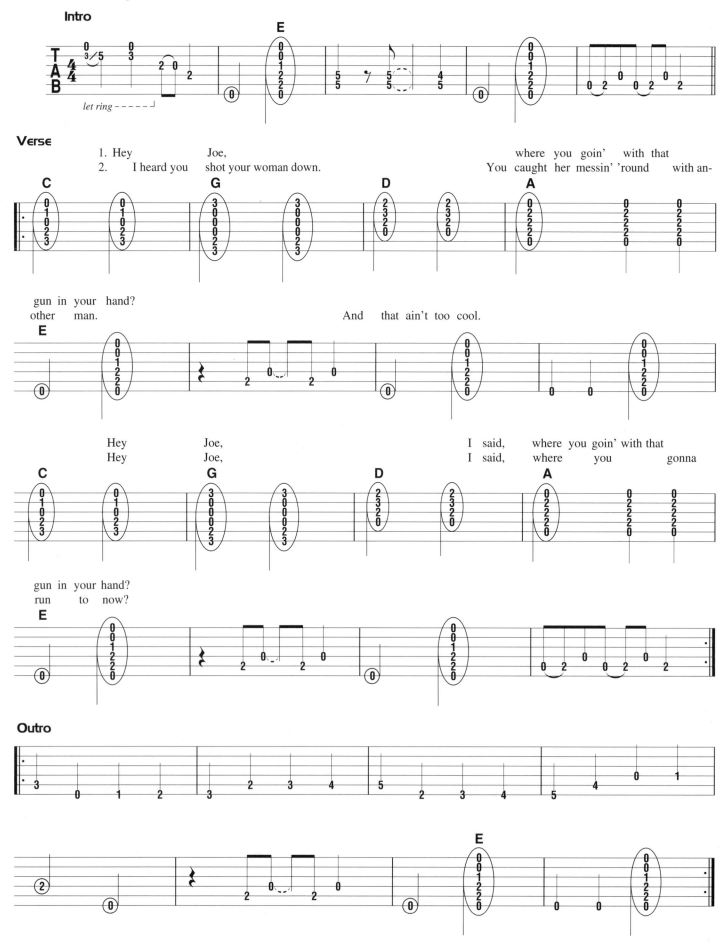

Words and Music by Billy Roberts
© 1962 (Renewed) by THIRD PALM MUSIC
All Rights Administered by BMG CHRYSALIS

CHECKPOINT

Congratulations, you've reached the halfway point of this method. Let's review some of what you've learned since the last Checkpoint.

CHORD NAMES

Draw a line to match each chord on the left with its correct name on the right.

     A

     E

     C

     Dm

     Am

     G

     D

     Em

SYMBOLS & TERMS

Draw a line to match each symbol on the left with its correct name on the right.

     Pull-Off

    Downstroke

𝄋   Repeat previous measure

∨   Upstroke

     D.S. Sign

⁒   Hammer-On

     Dyad

     Slide

Write the note names in the spaces provided.

A

Add bar lines.

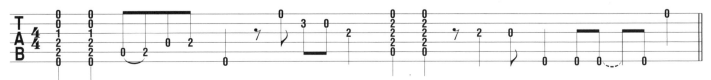

MOVIN' UP THE FRETBOARD

In Book One, we learned all of the notes within the first five frets. Now, as we start Book Two, let's move beyond first position and start playing "up the neck." Here are the notes within frets 5–12 on the low three strings.

SUNSHINE OF YOUR LOVE

Eric Clapton played the immortal riff in this song with the band Cream. Use your 3rd finger to fret the first note. Then, for the final three notes, shift down two frets to use your 3rd finger (low D) and 1st finger (F).

RUNNIN' DOWN A DREAM

Use **alternate picking** to play this Tom Petty riff up to speed. This simply means to alternate between downstrokes ( ) and upstrokes ( ). For this riff, start with an upstroke.

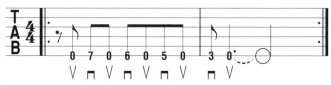

MISIRLOU

This Dick Dale surf-rock classic is fun to play on the low E string. Experiment with different fingerings, and use alternate picking to help you play more quickly. After you pick the last note, quickly slide your fret-hand finger down the string (to no particular fret).

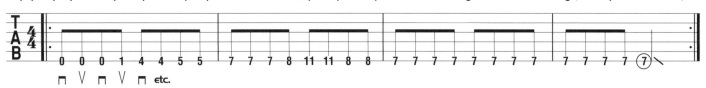

DON'T STOP BELIEVIN'

Here's a riff by the band Journey that jumps between two areas of the fretboard. Notice that the same note can be played at different locations. The last note of the 1st measure is the same low B as the first note of the 2nd measure.

I HATE MYSELF FOR LOVING YOU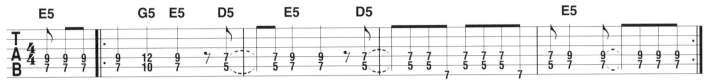

Power chords can be played "up the neck," too. The same two-finger shape is named by where the 1st finger is positioned. Here's a popular riff from the 1980s that features power chords with roots along the 5th string. Fret the 6th-string notes with your middle finger.

JESSIE'S GIRL

Rick Springfield's #1 hit provides more power chord practice.

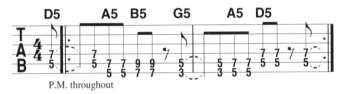

P.M. throughout

ROCK YOU LIKE A HURRICANE

The German hard rock group Scorpions used power chords for this popular rock anthem.

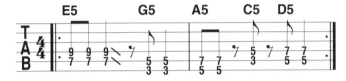

TALK DIRTY TO ME

This famous intro by the band Poison makes use of a common rhythm guitar technique known as **muffled strings**, or "scratches." When you see X's in tab, lift your fret-hand fingers just enough to prevent the notes from sounding. A percussive, "dead" sound will then result as you pick the strings.

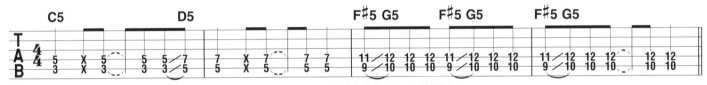

You've already learned that a dot after a note increases the value by one half. Therefore a **dotted quarter note** lasts for 1-1/2 beats.

WHEREVER I MAY ROAM

Now let's mix notes and power chords all along the fretboard with hammer-ons, slides, and dotted quarter notes.

MOVIN' UP THE FRETBOARD: PART 2

Here are the notes within frets 5–12 on the high three strings.

PURPLE HAZE 🔊

Jimi Hendrix's legendary riff is a must-know for all guitarists. For the first four notes, use fingers 3, 1, 2, and 1, respectively.

GET READY 🔊

This driving Motown hit makes good use of **double stops** (or dyads), which is a term borrowed from violin technique that means to pick two notes together. Flatten your finger to depress both notes simultaneously.

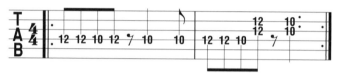

UP AROUND THE BEND 🔊

Here's a famous guitar intro by Creedence Clearwater Revival. Use your 2nd finger to play the slides and notes on the 3rd string, and lay your 1st finger across the top two strings to fret the notes at the 10th and 5th frets. Slide into the notes quickly from no particular starting point.

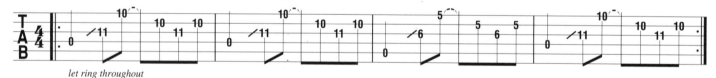

let ring throughout

MAMA, I'M COMING HOME 🔊

Guitarist Zakk Wylde played the descending guitar riff on this Ozzy Osbourne song. Arch your fingers and play on the tips to allow the open strings to ring out.

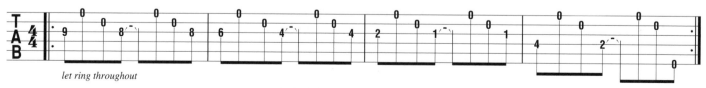

let ring throughout

THE MUNSTERS THEME 🔊

The sinister-sounding melody from this TV sitcom is fun to play, and provides more practice for playing "up" the neck.

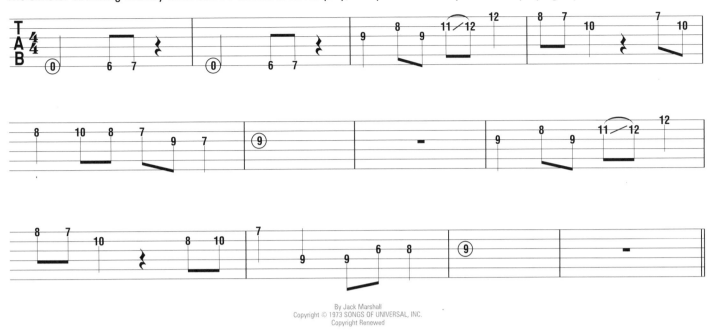

By Jack Marshall
Copyright © 1973 SONGS OF UNIVERSAL, INC.
Copyright Renewed

HAWAII FIVE-O THEME 🔊

Here's another popular TV tune. It was an instrumental hit for the Ventures in 1969, and is still often heard at sporting events. This one moves quickly, so be sure to use alternate picking.

By Mort Stevens
Copyright © 1969 Sony/ATV Music Publishing LLC and Aspenfair Music
Copyright Renewed
All Rights Administered by Sony/ATV Music Publishing LLC, 8 Music Square West, Nashville, TN 37203

HE'S A PIRATE

The theme from the movie series *Pirates of the Caribbean* is played in 3/4 time. Once again, use alternate picking for the eighth notes. Also, be sure to apply vibrato when it's notated.

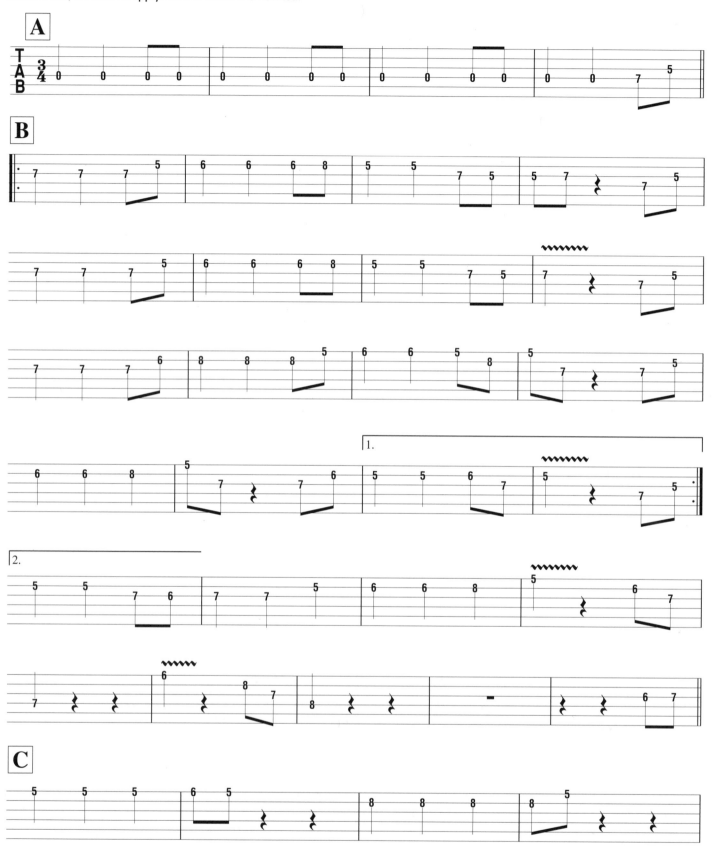

from Walt Disney Pictures' PIRATES OF THE CARIBBEAN: THE CURSE OF THE BLACK PEARL
Music by Klaus Badelt
© 2003 Walt Disney Music Company

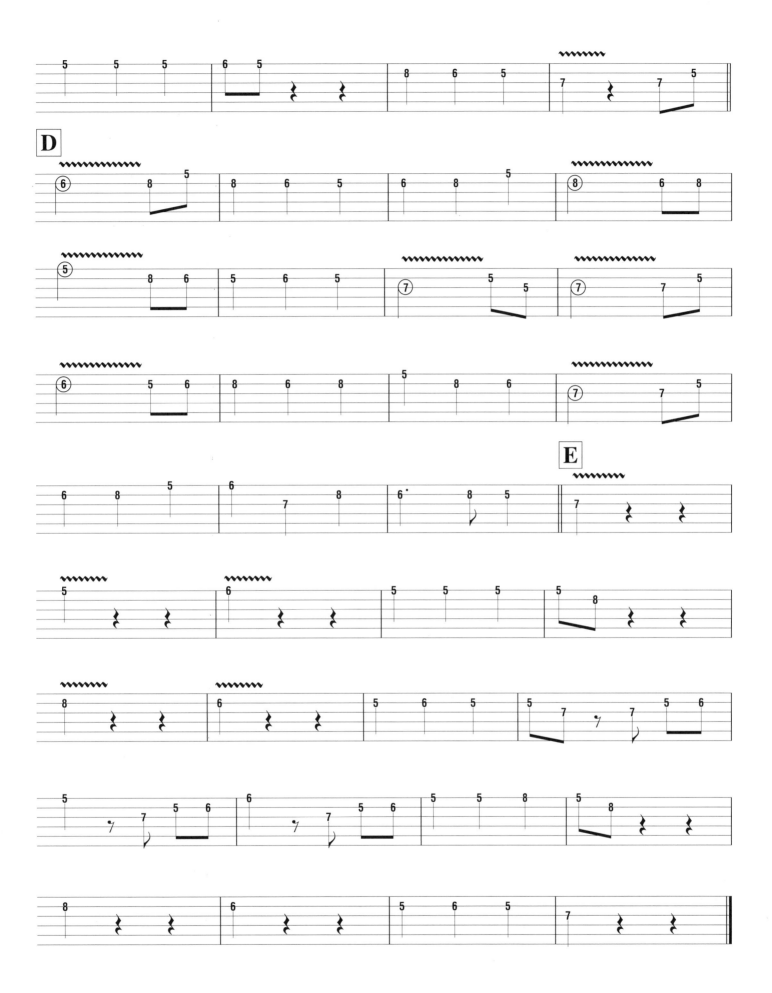

NEW RHYTHMS

A **sixteenth note** lasts half as long as an eighth note, and is written with two flags or two beams. There are four sixteenth notes in one beat.

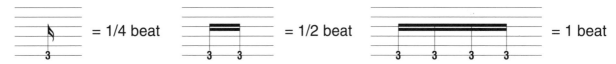

HELTER SKELTER

The raucous intro to this song by the Beatles uses sixteenth notes. Divide the beat into four, and count "one-e-and-a, two-e-and-a, three-e-and-a, four-e-and-a."

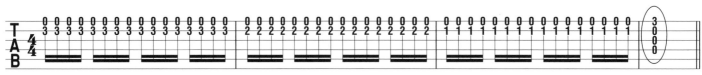

Count: 1-e-and-a 2-e-and-a etc.

Words and Music by John Lennon and Paul McCartney
Copyright © 1968 Sony/ATV Music Publishing LLC
Copyright Renewed
All Rights Administered by Sony/ATV Music Publishing LLC, 8 Music Square West, Nashville, TN 37203

I DON'T KNOW

Ready for some faster picking? Play the sixteenth notes on the open A string using steady, alternating downstrokes and upstrokes. Also apply palm muting to sound more like the original Ozzy Osbourne recording.

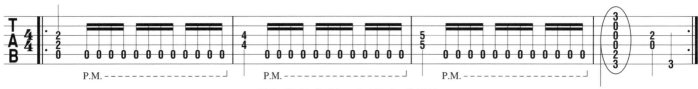

Words and Music by Ozzy Osbourne, Randy Rhoads and Bob Daisley
Copyright © 1981 Blizzard Music Limited, 12 Thayer Street, London, W1M 5LD, England

ROCK LOBSTER

Here's a fun riff by the B-52's. The second beat mixes an eighth note and two sixteenths.

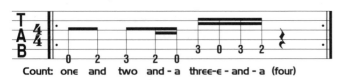

Count: one and two and - a three-e - and - a (four)

Words and Music by Kate Pierson, Fred Schneider, Keith Strickland, Cindy Wilson and Ricky Wilson
© 1979 EMI BLACKWOOD MUSIC INC., BOO FANT TUNES, INC. and DISTILLED MUSIC INC.
All Rights for BOO FANT TUNES, INC. Controlled and Administered by EMI BLACKWOOD MUSIC INC.

PLUSH

This song by Stone Temple Pilots features one of the most recognizable riffs of the 1990s.

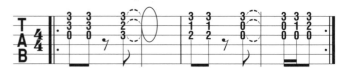

Words and Music by Scott Weiland, Dean DeLeo, Robert DeLeo and Eric Kretz
Copyright © 1992 MILKSONGS and TRIPLE KAUF NO PLATE MUZAK
All Rights for MILKSONGS Controlled and Administered by UNIVERSAL MUSIC CORP.
All Rights for TRIPLE KAUF NO PLATE MUZAK Administered by BMG RIGHTS MANAGEMENT (US) LLC

THE TROOPER

Use pull-offs to help you play Iron Maiden's signature riff up to full speed.

Words and Music by Steven Harris
Copyright © 1996 by Iron Maiden Holdings Ltd.
All Rights in the United States and Canada Administered by Universal Music - Z Tunes LLC

THE JOKER

This song by the Steve Miller Band was a #1 hit in 1974.

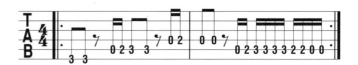

Words and Music by Steve Miller, Eddie Curtis and Ahmet Ertegun
Copyright © 1973 by Sailor Music, Jim Rooster Music and Warner-Tamerlane Publishing Corp.
Copyright Renewed
All Rights for Jim Rooster Music Administered Worldwide by Sailor Music

THEME FROM KING OF THE HILL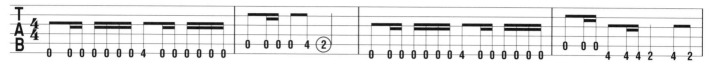

The galloping guitar riff in the theme from this animated TV series sounds cool and also serves as a great picking exercise.

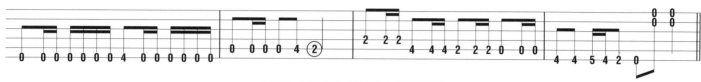

IRON MAN

Now let's try sixteenths with power chords in Black Sabbath's all-time classic metal track.

MY BEST FRIEND'S GIRL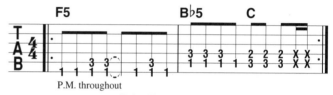

This riff by the Cars uses muffled sixteenths in transition from the C dyad back to F.

SOUTH OF HEAVEN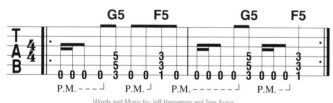

For a fuller sound, power chords can be expanded to three notes. Try playing the reinforced shape on this riff by the band Slayer.

AMERICAN WOMAN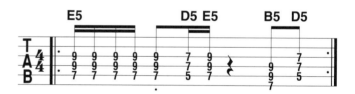

The Guess Who's #1 hit also puts three-note power chords to good use.

BARRACUDA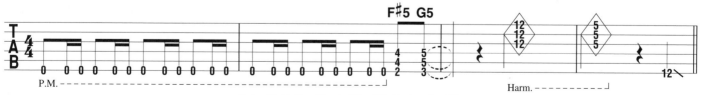

The hard rock song "Barracuda" is the band Heart's signature song. Its aggressive opening riff uses sixteenth notes and **natural harmonics**. When you see "Harm." under the tab and diamonds around the tab numbers, pick the strings while the fret-hand lightly touches the strings directly over the metal fret wire. Natural harmonics produce bell-like, chiming tones.

CHANGES

Jimi Hendrix recorded this song on the famous live album, *Band of Gypsys*. Two of the guitar riffs are repeated several times. To avoid tabbing the same parts over and over again, riffs and/or rhythm figures are often labeled and recalled.

Intro

Repeat previous two measures

Riff A

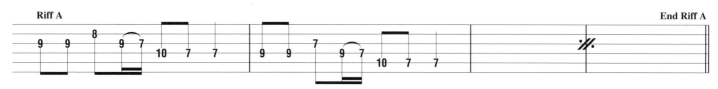

End Riff A

1. Well, my
2. Well, my

Riff B

End Riff B

Verse

w/ Riff B (4 times)

| mind | is goin' through them | changes, | | I feel just like I'm hyp - no - | tized. |
| mind | is goin' through them | changes, | | I think I'm goin' out of my | mind. |

| Every | time | you | see | me | goin' somewhere, | | I think I'm goin' out of my | mind, yeah. |
| Every | time | you | see | me | goin' somewhere, | | I think I could commit a | crime, now. |

| Oh, | my baby, she left | me | the other day, | | and we were havin' so much | fun, yeah, yeah. |
| She | had me runnin', | she | had me cryin'. | | She had me runnin', had me, | had me, had me cryin'. |

| Oh, | my baby, she stepped | out on me, | | and that's the reason why she | had me cryin'. |
| She had me runnin', | she had me cryin'. | | She had me runnin', had... |

Chorus

w/ Riff A

It's alright oh, yeah, yeah. It's alright.

Words and Music by George "Buddy" Miles
© 1967 (Renewed) MILES AHEAD MUSIC (ASCAP)

A **triplet** is a group of three notes played in the space of two. Whereas eighth notes divide a beat into two parts, **eighth-note triplets** divide a beat into three parts.

 = 1 beat

ADDAMS FAMILY THEME

While playing the riff from this classic TV show, count your new rhythm by simply saying the word "tri-pl-et."

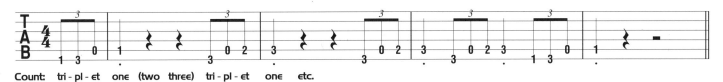

Count: tri - pl - et   one (two three) tri - pl - et   one   etc.

Theme from the TV Show and Movie
Music and Lyrics by Vic Mizzy
Copyright © 1964, Renewed 1992 by Unison Music Company
Administered by Next Decade Entertainment, Inc.

AM I EVIL?

Triplets fuel the menacing sound of this riff. Metallica's famous cover version is considered one of the heaviest metal tracks ever.

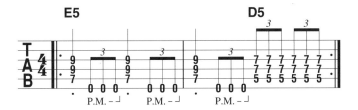

Words and Music by Sean Harris and Brian Tatler
Copyright © 1979 by Imagem London Ltd.
All Rights in the United States and Canada Administered by Universal Music - Z Tunes LLC

SPANISH BOLERO

Musicians from Maurice Ravel to Jeff Beck have made use of this rhythm. The chord movement is easy; just slide the open E chord shape.

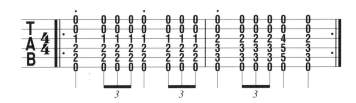

Copyright © 2012 by HAL LEONARD CORPORATION

JESU, JOY OF MAN'S DESIRING

Here's a well-known classical piece that uses triplets in 3/4 time.

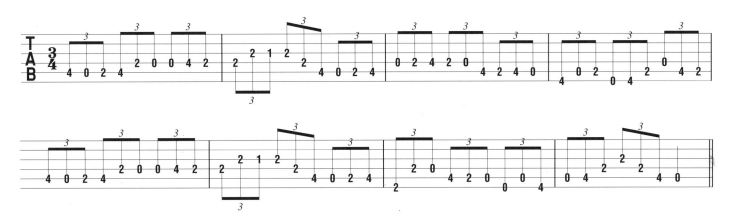

By Johann Sebastian Bach
Copyright © 2012 by HAL LEONARD CORPORATION

A **shuffle** is a bouncy, skipping rhythm. Eighth notes are played as long-short, rather than as equal values. The feel is the same as inserting a rest in the middle of a triplet.

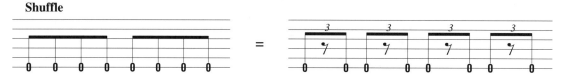

YOU SHOOK ME

Muddy Waters, Led Zeppelin, and others recorded this popular blues song.

PRIDE AND JOY

Here's the main riff of blues guitar hero Stevie Ray Vaughan's signature song. Use alternate picking.

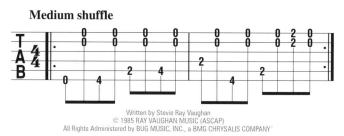

THE BOYS ARE BACK IN TOWN

Now let's mix shuffled eighth notes and triplets to play a rock classic by Thin Lizzy.

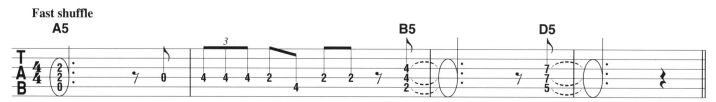

THAT'LL BE THE DAY

This Buddy Holly hit is one of early rock 'n' roll's most enduring songs.

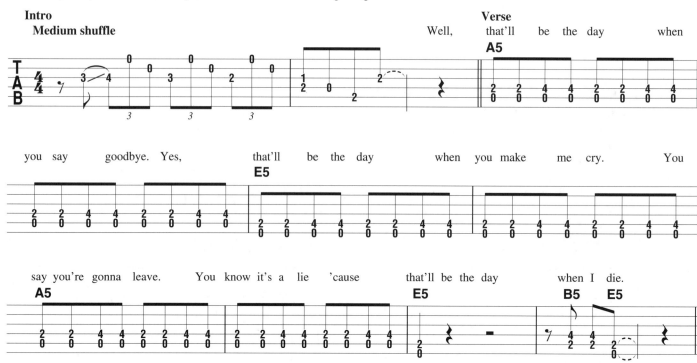

THE PINK PANTHER

Henry Mancini was one of the greatest composers of the 20th century. "The Pink Panther" is a shuffle that uses triplets, pull-offs, slides, and notes on all six strings.

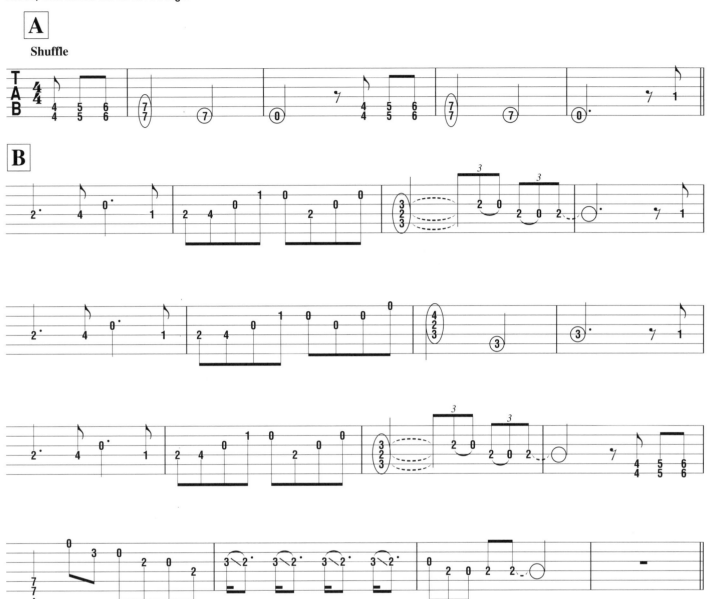

By Henry Mancini
Copyright © 1964 NORTHRIDGE MUSIC CO. and EMI U CATALOG INC.
Copyright Renewed
All Rights for NORTHRIDGE MUSIC CO. Controlled and Administered by UNIVERSAL MUSIC CORP.

A **quarter-note triplet** divides two beats into three equal parts. In other words, the three quarter notes in this triplet equal the same time as two regular quarter notes.

 = 2 beats

SEVEN NATION ARMY

Observe the counting below the tab of this riff by the White Stripes.

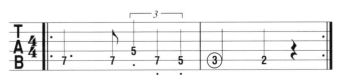

Count: one two and tri-pl-et   one two three (four)

Words and Music by Jack White
Copyright © 2002 Peppermint Stripe Music (BMI)

HOLD THE LINE

The band Toto scored their first hit with "Hold the Line."

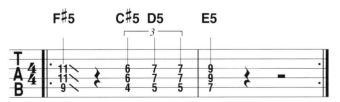

Words and Music by David Paich
Copyright © 1978 Hudmar Publishing Co., Inc.
All Rights Controlled and Administered by Spirit Two Music, Inc.

DETROIT ROCK CITY

Now try your hand at playing another full song. Here's a vintage favorite by the band Kiss.

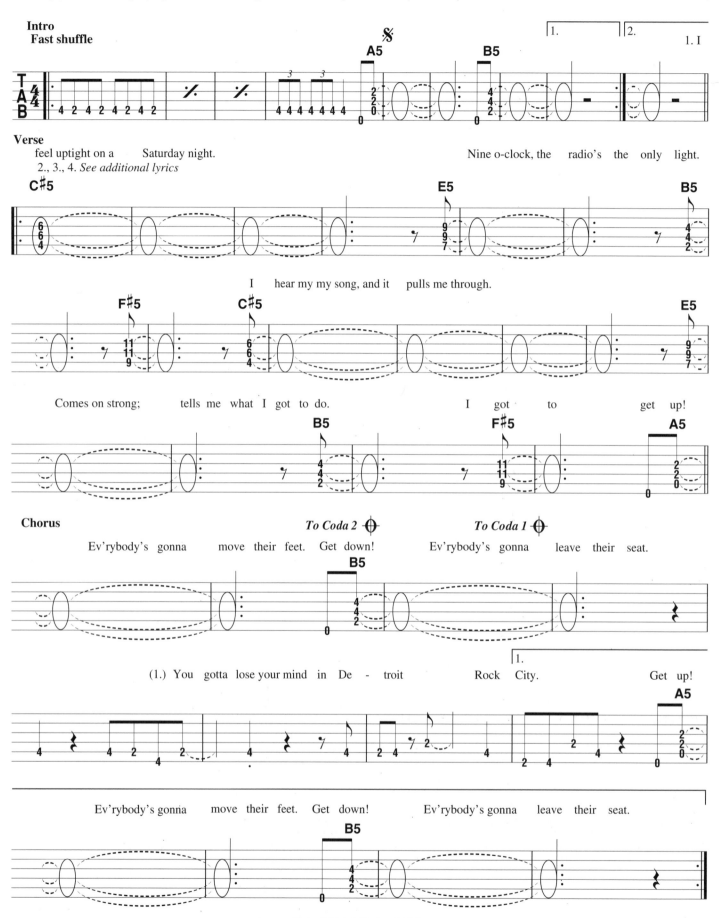

Intro
Fast shuffle

Verse

feel uptight on a   Saturday night.

2., 3., 4. *See additional lyrics*

Nine o-clock, the   radio's the   only   light.

I   hear my my song, and it   pulls me through.

Comes on strong;   tells me what I got to do.   I   got   to   get up!

Chorus

To Coda 2 ⊕   *To Coda 1* ⊕

Ev'rybody's gonna   move their feet. Get down!   Ev'rybody's gonna   leave   their   seat.

(1.) You gotta lose your mind in De - troit   Rock City.   Get up!

Ev'rybody's gonna   move their feet. Get down!   Ev'rybody's gonna   leave   their   seat.

Words and Music by Paul Stanley and Bob Ezrin

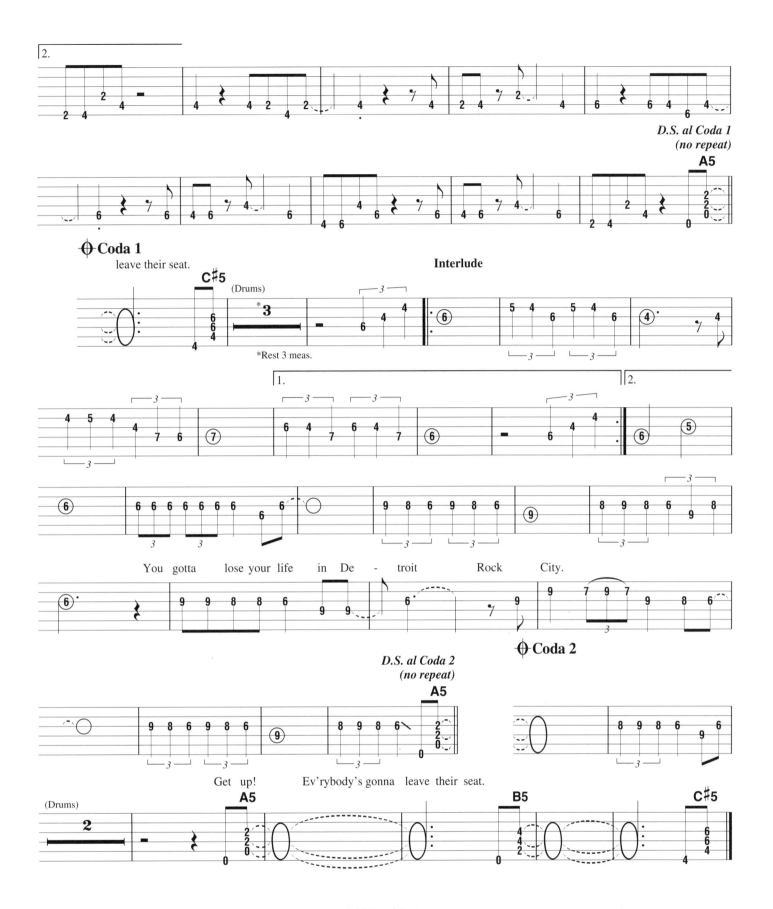

Additional Lyrics

2. Gettin' late, I just can't wait.
   Ten o'clock, and I know I gotta hit the road.
   First I drink, then I smoke.
   Start up the car,
   And I try to make the midnight show. Get up!

3. Movin' fast down Ninety-Five.
   I hit top speed,
   But I'm still movin' much too slow.
   I feel so good; I'm so alive.
   Hear my song playin' on the radio.
   It goes: get up!

4. Twelve o'clock, I gotta rock.
   There's a truck ahead,
   Lights starin' at my eyes.
   Whoa, my God, no time to turn.
   I got to laugh, 'cause I know I'm gonna die.
   Why? Get up!

THE MAJOR SCALE

A **scale** is a succession of notes ascending or descending in a specific order. The most common scale is the **major scale**. It can be built starting on any root note, and follows a specific pattern of **whole steps** (two frets) and **half steps** (one fret). Here it is beginning on the low E.

E MAJOR SCALE

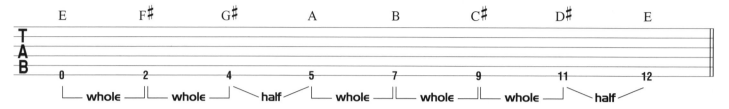

Although it's easy to visualize the scale pattern across one string, it's not practical to play it this way. Here is the standard fingering for playing the major scale on the guitar.

G MAJOR SCALE

The scale above starts on the note G, so it's a G major scale. If you move the pattern up two frets, it becomes an A major scale.

A MAJOR SCALE

You can apply this movable major scale pattern to any root note along the low string. The pattern should be practiced, with alternate picking, ascending and descending.

Here's another way to visualize the movable pattern:

Major Scale Pattern 1 – Root on 6th String

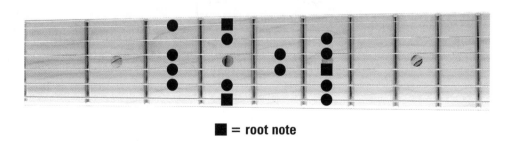

■ = root note

Practicing scales is a good way to develop fret-hand technique. Start slowly, and gradually build up speed.

The notes of the major scale are the foundation for countless melodies, riffs, solos, and chord progressions. Here are a few examples.

DO-RE-MI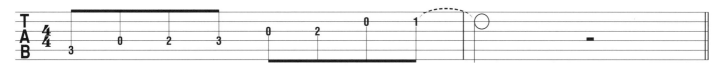

This Rodgers and Hammerstein song from *The Sound of Music* is arguably the most famous use of the major scale in popular music. The lyrics also teach the seven solfège syllables commonly used to sing the major scale. The melody uses mostly notes from the C major scale, and shifts briefly to D major and E major in measures 11 and 13, respectively.

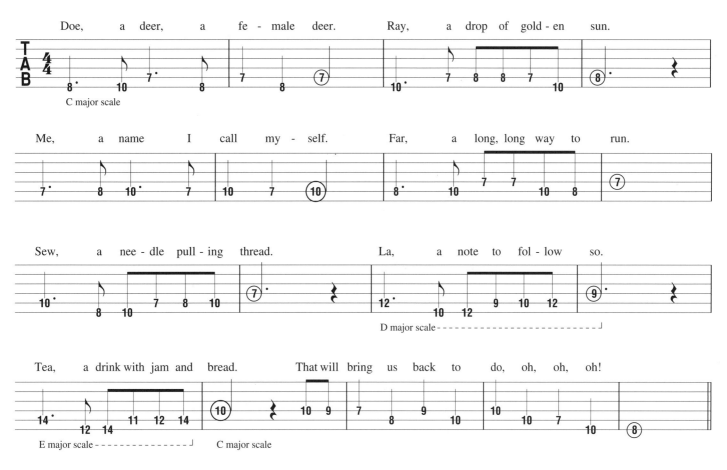

HELLO, GOODBYE

The main riff in the chorus of this song by the Beatles runs straight up the C major scale, tabbed here in open position.

There are many patterns for playing the major scale on the guitar. Here's one with three notes per string that has its root on the 5th string. Let's try it in D.

D MAJOR SCALE

	D	E	F#	G	A	B	C#	D	E	F#	G	A	B	C#	D
Fret-hand fingers:	1	2	4	1	2	4	1	2	4	1	2	4	1	3	4

To help you visualize the pattern, here it is on the fretboard:

Major Scale Pattern 2 – Root on 5th String

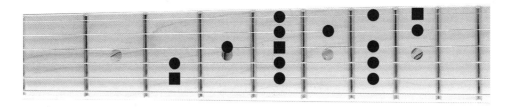

■ = root note

JOY TO THE WORLD 🔊

The melody of this famous Christmas carol, by Baroque composer George Frideric Handel, uses all of the notes in the D major scale.

Words by Isaac Watts
Music by George Frideric Handel
Adapted by Lowell Mason

MUSIC THEORY 101

When we see that the notes of a particular song come from a certain scale, we say that the song is in the **key** of that scale. For instance, if the notes of a song all come from the C major scale, we say that the song is in the key of C major.

GOODBYE TO ROMANCE 🔊

The intro to "Goodbye to Romance" by Ozzy Osbourne uses notes exclusively from the D major scale:

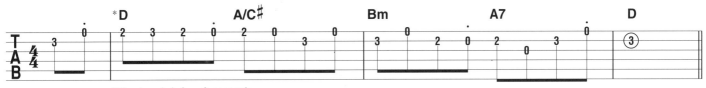

*Chord symbols for reference only.

Words and Music by John Osbourne, Robert Daisley and Randy Rhoads
TRO - © Copyright 1981 and 1984 Essex Music International, Inc., New York and Blizzard Music, Daytona Beach, FL

Notice how the guitar part seems to be "at rest" when you arrive at the last note (D)? This is because the D note is the root, or **tonic**—the note around which the key revolves.

MAJOR SCALE CHART

Major scales are the building blocks of music, and music theory. Chords and chord progressions are also derived from scales. Following is a handy table that spells the notes in all 12 keys. Don't get bogged down trying to memorize all this at once, but you might want to dog-ear this page for future reference.

	1 (root)	2	3	4	5	6	7
C major	C	D	E	F	G	A	B
G major	G	A	B	C	D	E	F#
D major	D	E	F#	G	A	B	C#
A major	A	B	C#	D	E	F#	G#
E major	E	F#	G#	A	B	C#	D#
B major	B	C#	D#	E	F#	G#	A#
F# major	F#	G#	A#	B	C#	D#	E#
D♭ major	D♭	E♭	F	G♭	A♭	B♭	C
A♭ major	A♭	B♭	C	D♭	E♭	F	G
E♭ major	E♭	F	G	A♭	B♭	C	D
B♭ major	B♭	C	D	E♭	F	G	A
F major	F	G	A	B♭	C	D	E

THE F CHORD

The F chord uses no open strings, and it also requires the use of a **barre** (pronounced "bar"). Barring is done by flattening a finger across more than one string at a time. Here, use your 1st finger to press down the 1st and 2nd strings. Adjust the angle of your finger, or rotate your finger slightly on its side as necessary, so the notes sound clearly. Fret the remaining two notes with your 2nd and 3rd fingers as shown.

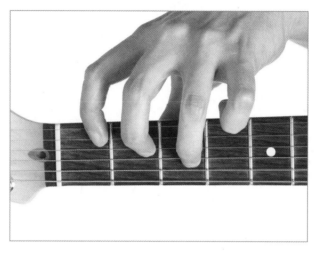

FREE BIRD

Let's take it slow with your new chord, and try playing it in the chord progression of Lynyrd Skynyrd's classic rock ballad.

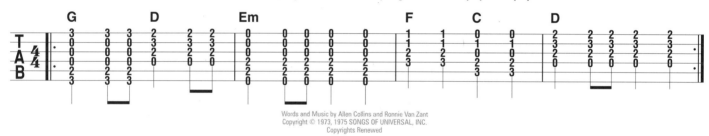

Words and Music by Allen Collins and Ronnie Van Zant
Copyright © 1973, 1975 SONGS OF UNIVERSAL, INC.
Copyrights Renewed

LEARNING TO FLY

Tom Petty's acoustic hit uses four chords, including F, in steady eighth-note strums.

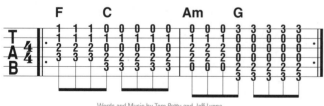

Words and Music by Tom Petty and Jeff Lynne
Copyright © 1991 Gone Gator Music and EMI April Music Inc.

FLY LIKE AN EAGLE

Steve Miller's 1977 hit can be played with just three chords: Am, D, and F. First try the tabbed strum pattern, and then try improvising your own right-hand strums.

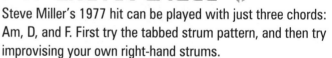
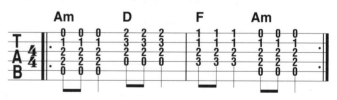

Words and Music by Steve Miller
Copyright © 1976 by Sailor Music
Copyright Renewed

LIKE A ROLLING STONE

Bob Dylan's iconic song is fun to strum. Again, feel free to vary your right-hand strumming as it feels natural to you.

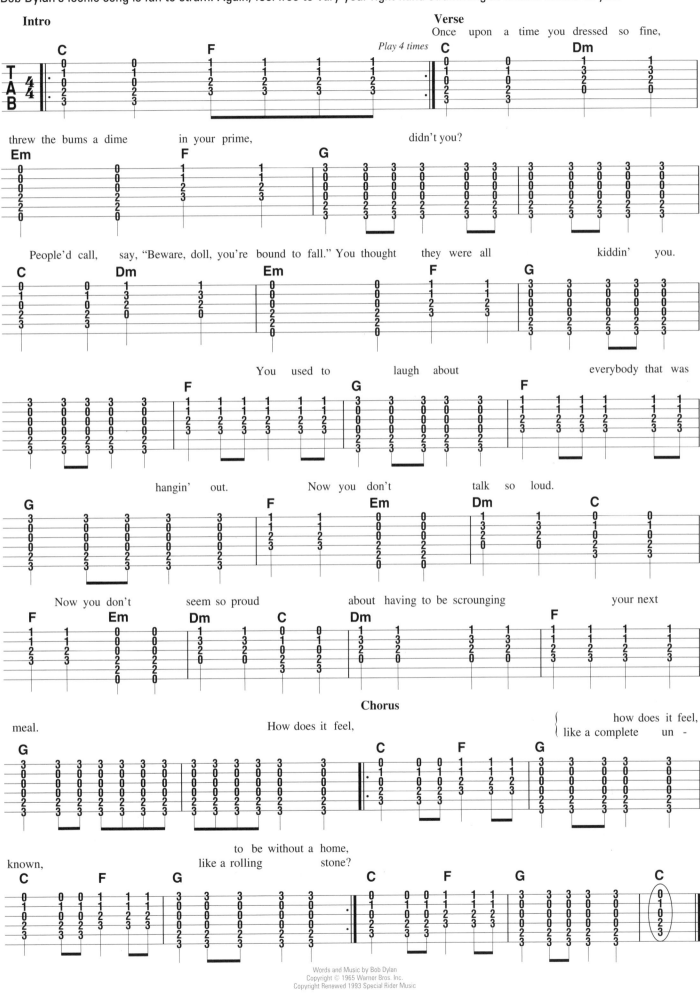

Words and Music by Bob Dylan
Copyright © 1965 Warner Bros. Inc.
Copyright Renewed 1993 Special Rider Music

SEVENTH CHORDS

Seventh chords are comprised of four different notes. They sound richer than ordinary major and minor chords that contain three notes, but are generally not more difficult to play. The most common type of seventh chord is the **dominant seventh**. It is built from the root, 3rd, 5th, and flat-7th **degrees** (notes) of the major scale, and its chord label simply includes the suffix "7."

E7

A7

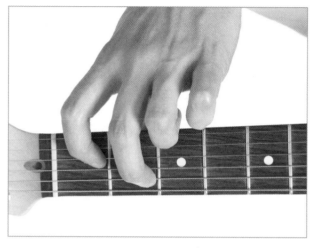

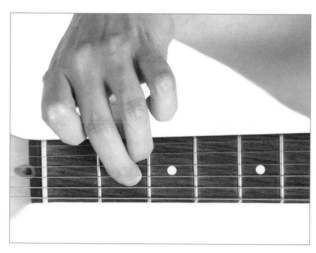

LOVE ME TENDER

Strum once per beat to play this #1 hit ballad by Elvis Presley.

Love me tender   love me sweet.   Never   let   me   go.
You have made my   life complete   and   I   love you   so.

TAKE ME TO THE RIVER

Al Green's 1974 hit has been recorded by many artists. Use your 1st finger to press (or barre) all the notes of the A chord in the song's main groove.

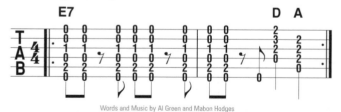

SMOOTH

Carlos Santana and Rob Thomas collaborated on this Latin-style, Grammy-winning hit. Here's the main chord progression.

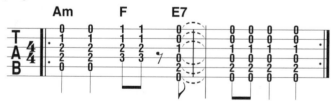

TWIST AND SHOUT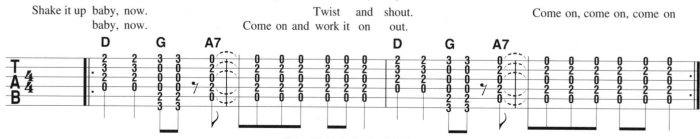

Now try a song recorded by the Beatles that changes chords more quickly.

Shake it up baby, now.   Twist   and   shout.   Come on, come on, come on
          baby, now.   Come on and work it on   out.

D7

G7

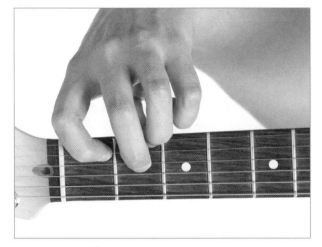

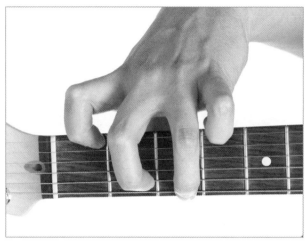

TAXMAN

This song by the Beatles features seventh chords played on the "backbeat," or beats 2 and 4 of most measures.

Let me   tell   you   how   it   will   be.   There's one
for   you,   nineteen   for   me.   'Cause I'm the

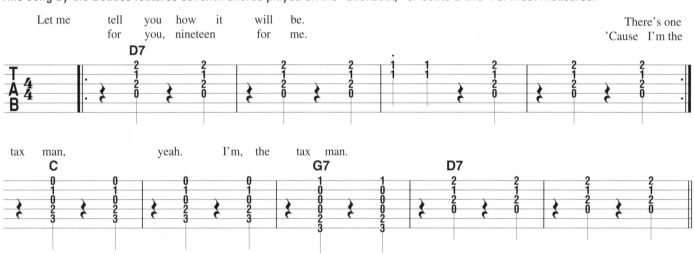

tax man,   yeah.   I'm, the   tax man.

Words and Music by George Harrison
Copyright © 1966 Sony/ATV Music Publishing LLC
Copyright Renewed
All Rights Administered by Sony/ATV Music Publishing LLC, 8 Music Square West, Nashville, TN 37203

FIVE FOOT TWO, EYES OF BLUE

The California Ramblers recorded the original version of this fun big band hit in 1925. Remember that a "shuffle" means to strum the eighth notes with a long-short feel.

Shuffle

1. Five foot   two,   eyes   of   blue,   but oh what those five   foot could do.
2. Turned up   nose,   turned down hose,   never   had   no   other beaus.   Has

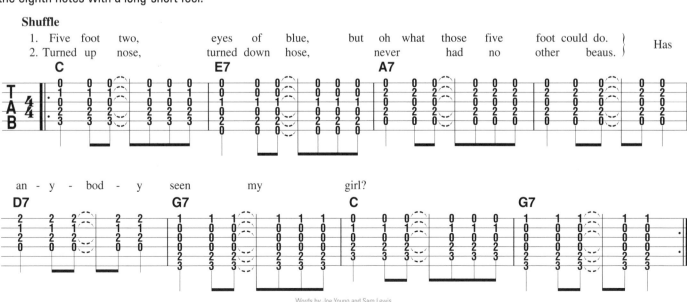

an-y-bod-y   seen   my   girl?

Words by Joe Young and Sam Lewis
Music by Ray Henderson
© 1925 LEO FEIST, INC.
© Renewed 1953 WAROCK CORP., LEO FEIST, INC. and HENDERSON MUSIC CO.
All Rights for LEO FEIST, INC. and HENDERSON MUSIC CO. in Canada Administered by REDWOOD MUSIC LTD.

ALL I WANNA DO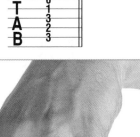

Sheryl Crow's breakthrough hit won a Grammy for "Record of the Year" in 1995.

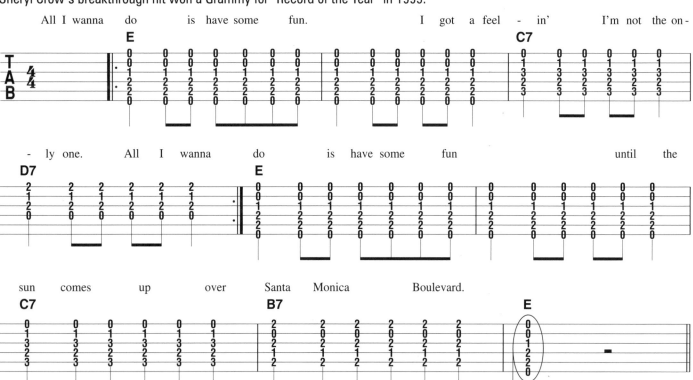

All I wanna do is have some fun. I got a feel - in' I'm not the on-
- ly one. All I wanna do is have some fun until the
sun comes up over Santa Monica Boulevard.

Words and Music by Kevin Gilbert, David Baerwald, Sheryl Crow, Wyn Cooper and Bill Bottrell
Copyright © 1993 Sony/ATV Music Publishing LLC, Almo Music Corp., Zen Of Iniquity, Warner-Tamerlane Publishing Corp., Old Crow Music, WB Music Corp., Canvas Mattress Music and Ignorant Music
All Rights on behalf of Sony/ATV Music Publishing LLC Administered by Sony/ATV Music Publishing LLC, 8 Music Square West, Nashville, TN 37203
All Rights on behalf of Zen Of Iniquity Administered by Almo Music Corp.

SGT. PEPPER'S LONELY HEARTS CLUB BAND

Guitarists often prefer to read from simple **chord charts** rather than follow each strum in tab. Try this approach with the Beatles' song below. Feel free to vary your strumming at will, or listen to the audio for a guide.

G7	A7	C7	G7
It was | twenty years ago today,	Sergeant | Pepper taught the band to play.		They've been

A7	C7	G7	A7
going in and out of style	but they're | guaranteed to raise a smile.	So | may I introduce to you	the

C7	G7	C7	G7
act you've known for all these years?	| Sergeant Pepper's	Lonely Hearts Club Band. |	

Words and Music by John Lennon and Paul McCartney
Copyright © 1967 Sony/ATV Music Publishing LLC
Copyright Renewed
All Rights Administered by Sony/ATV Music Publishing LLC, 8 Music Square West, Nashville, TN 37203

I SAW HER STANDING THERE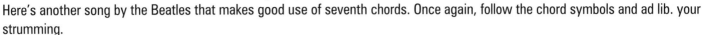

Here's another song by the Beatles that makes good use of seventh chords. Once again, follow the chord symbols and ad lib. your strumming.

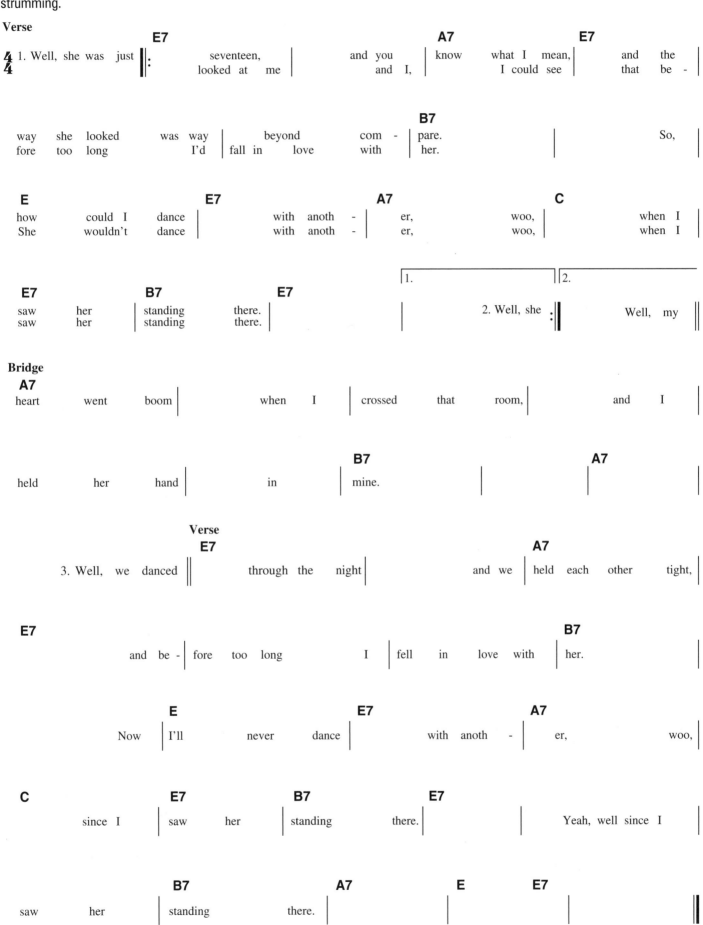

6/8 TIME

A **6/8 time signature** means there are six beats in each measure, and an eighth note receives one beat. All note and rest values are proportionate to the eighth note. In other words, a quarter note receives two beats, a sixteenth note receives a half beat, and so on. Traditionally, in 6/8 time, the 1st and 4th beats are emphasized.

LUCY IN THE SKY WITH DIAMONDS

The instrumental melody in the intro of this song by the Beatles is a good example of 6/8 time. Observe the counting below the tab.

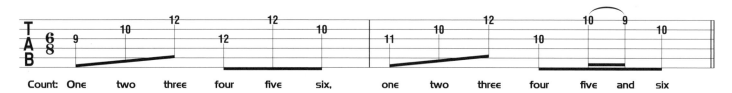

I'M SHIPPING UP TO BOSTON

This Irish jig by the Celtic punk band Dropkick Murphys is popular at sporting events. Chord symbols are included above the staff for reference.

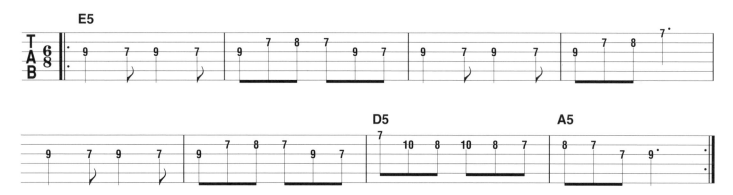

ELDERLY WOMAN BEHIND THE COUNTER IN A SMALL TOWN

Here's a Pearl Jam song in 6/8 that uses common variations of the ordinary C and G chords. The new C chord is technically called "Cadd9" because the 9th (D) is added to the basic chord. The new G chord is just an alternate voicing; instead of the open 2nd string (B), the note D is played at the 3rd fret. The new C and G chords are handy because both use the 3rd and 4th fingers to press the same notes on strings 2 and 1, respectively.

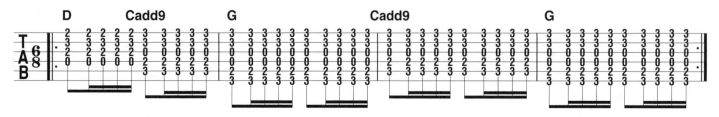

PICKING CHORDS

Strumming isn't your only option when playing chords; another way to play chords is by picking them, one note at a time. This approach offers a lighter accompaniment and works nicely for ballads.

EVERYBODY HURTS

For R.E.M.'s "Everybody Hurts," use consecutive downstrokes ( ) when picking the chords low to high, and consecutive upstrokes ( ) when picking high to low. Keep all the notes of each chord depressed so they ring together.

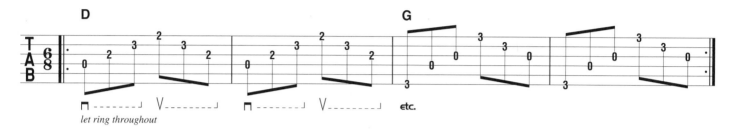

HALLELUJAH

Leonard Cohen's haunting ballad has been covered many times. The picking pattern includes the note F♯ to connect the two chords in the main progression.

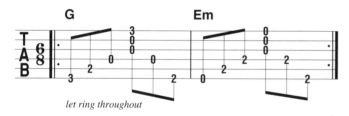

BRAIN DAMAGE

Pink Floyd's song from the classic album *Dark Side of the Moon* combines chord strums and picking.

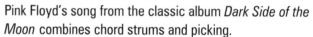
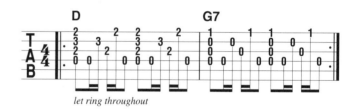

THE HOUSE OF THE RISING SUN

The Animals' version of the folk classic charted in two decades, and features one of the most memorable guitar intros of all time.

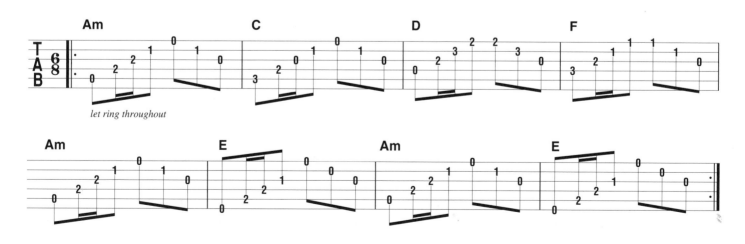

THE MINOR PENTATONIC SCALE

Now that you can play chords, riffs, and rhythms, it's time to try some lead guitar. The **minor pentatonic scale** is made up of five notes, and is the scale most commonly used to create rock and blues solos. Here is the scale's movable finger pattern, which guitarists often refer to as "box position."

Minor Pentatonic Scale Pattern 1 – Root on 6th String

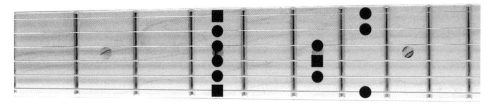

■ = root note

The pattern above can be transposed, or moved up or down the neck and played in any key. If you start the pattern with your 1st finger on the 5th fret (low A), you're playing an A minor pentatonic scale. If you move down to the 1st fret (low F), it's F minor pentatonic.

A MINOR PENTATONIC

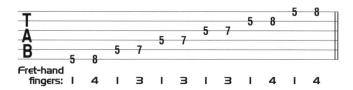

Fret-hand fingers: 1 4 1 3 1 3 1 3 1 4 1 4

F MINOR PENTATONIC

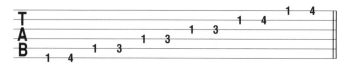

A **lick** is a short, self-contained phrase. Lead guitarists combine memorized and/or improvised licks to form a solo. Here are a few common licks derived from the minor pentatonic scale.

LICK #1

This repeating lick, based in A minor pentatonic, is a favorite of Eric Clapton.

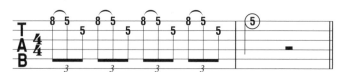

LICK #2

Here's one in the style of Led Zeppelin's Jimmy Page, also rooted in A.

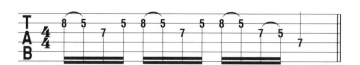

LICK #3

Now let's move the "box" pattern to C (8th fret) for a lick in the style of Texas blues great Freddie King.

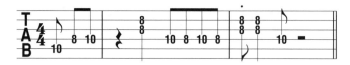

LICK #4

Rock 'n' roll legend Chuck Berry often used double stops in his solos, similar to this phrase in D.

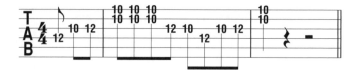

THEORY TIP							
The minor pentatonic scale is built from the root, flat-3rd, 4th, 5th, and flat-7th degrees of the major scale.							
C major scale =	C	D	E	F	G	A	B
	1		♭3	4	5		♭7
C minor pentatonic scale =	C		E♭	F	G		B♭

BENDING STRINGS

The **string bend** is a legato technique that produces an emotional, vocal-like sound. The fret-hand fingers push or pull the string out of its normal alignment, stretching it so the pitch of the note is raised.

Follow the steps and tab below to play your first bend. It is called a **whole-step bend** because the sound is raised to match the pitch you normally get two frets higher.

- Depress the note at the 7th fret with your 3rd finger.

- Place your 1st and 2nd fingers on the same string for support, then hook your thumb around the top of the neck for leverage.

- Pick the 3rd string and, while maintaining pressure, push "up" towards the ceiling.

Whole-Step Bend

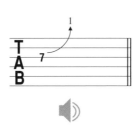

TIN PAN ALLEY
The intro to this Stevie Ray Vaughan slow blues is played in the B minor pentatonic box position.

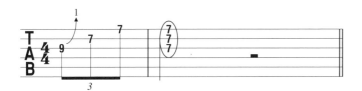

LA GRANGE
Use your 3rd or 4th finger to bend the 2nd string in this C minor pentatonic lick, which opens the solo to this ZZ Top classic.

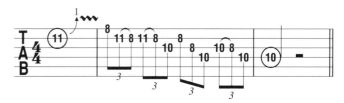

CAN'T BUY ME LOVE
Guitarist George Harrison played the solo on the Beatles' "Can't Buy Me Love" in the C minor pentatonic box position. His lead includes a **bend and release**. Pick the note, bend it, and maintain pressure as you lower the bend (without re-picking) back to its original pitch.

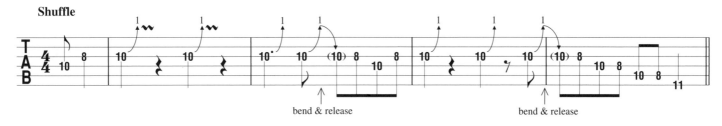

YOU GIVE LOVE A BAD NAME 🔊

The lead guitar melody in this Bon Jovi hit features a pull-off following a bend and release in the 4th measure. All of the notes are drawn from the standard C minor pentatonic box (8th fret).

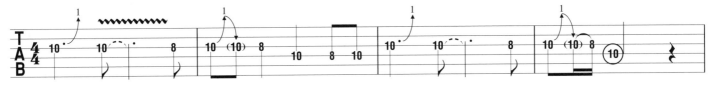

WONDERFUL TONIGHT 🔊

Eric Clapton's popular ballad features another lead melody that is great for practicing the whole-step bend and release. Listen carefully to be sure you accurately bend the note on the 10th fret (A) to match the pitch on the 12th fret (B). This example is not derived from the minor pentatonic; it uses notes from the G major scale.

The **half-step bend** raises the pitch of a note to match the note one fret higher. The bend is played in the same manner as the whole-step bend; the string is simply not pushed quite as far.

BIRTHDAY 🔊

Here's another classic riff by the Beatles. Bend the F♯ note on the 2nd string to match the pitch of G.

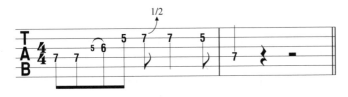

BANG A GONG (GET IT ON) 🔊

Most bends are done on the first three thinner strings, but it's not uncommon to bend the low strings. For this riff by the band T. Rex, use your 2nd finger to pull the string downward, or towards the floor.

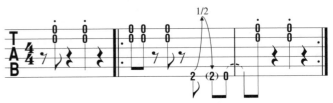

STILL GOT THE BLUES 🔊

Now let's combine whole- and half-step bends. Here is the theme to guitar great Gary Moore's poignant blues ballad.

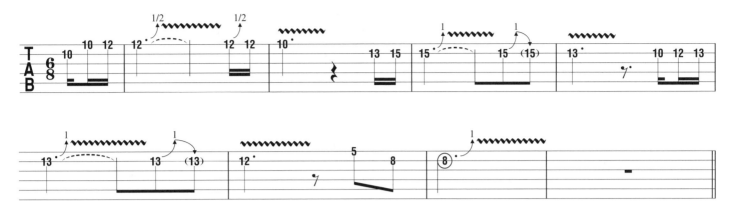

The **quarter-step bend** works well on any string and can add taste and style to a lead lick or lower-register riff. Sometimes called a "smear," this one can be played with any finger without reinforcement.

THE THRILL IS GONE 🔊

Master bluesman B.B. King plays the intro lead of his signature song using notes from the B minor pentatonic scale. He also goes beyond the basic box and extends the scale pattern with notes on the 12th fret of the 1st and 2nd strings. His mixture of quarter-, half-, and whole-step bends really makes the solo sing (and cry).

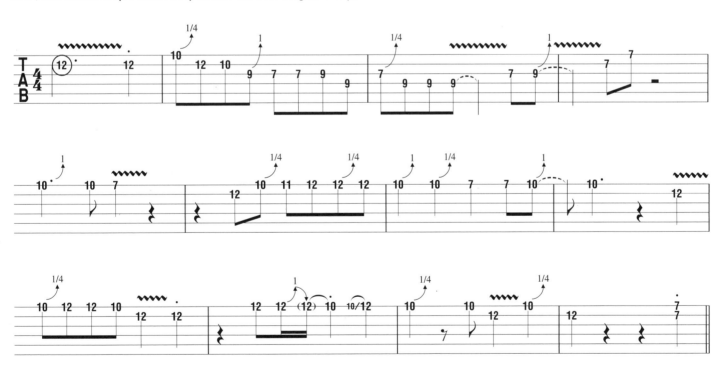

SLEEPWALK

Guitarists Jeff Beck, Larry Carlton, Joe Satriani, and Brian Setzer have recorded this instrumental hit.

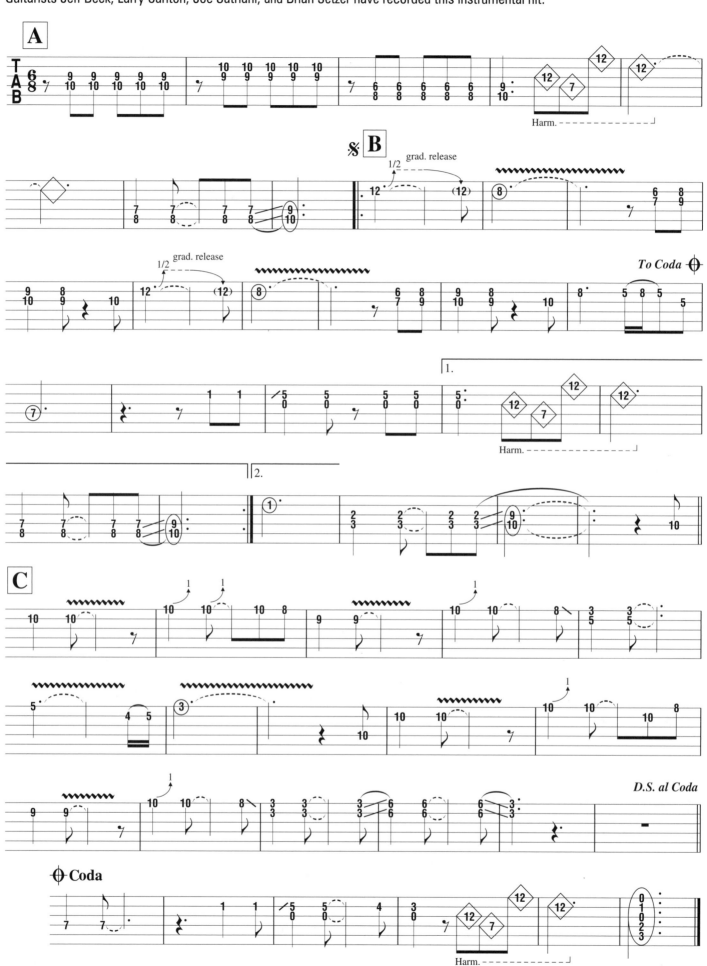

CHECKPOINT

You have successfully completed the *Hal Leonard Guitar Tab Method*. Well done! Let's go over a few of the notes, terms, and rhythms covered since the last Checkpoint.

NOTE NAMES

Draw a line to match each note on the left with its correct name on the right.

F

F#

A

C

E♭

D♭

B

E

SYMBOLS & TERMS

Draw a line to match each symbol on the left with its correct name on the right.

Natural Harmonics

Quarter-Note Triplet

Sixteenth Note

Muffled Strings

Double Stops

Dotted Quarter Note

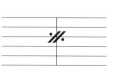

Eighth-Note Triplet

Repeat previous two measures

Write the note names in the spaces provided.

Add bar lines.

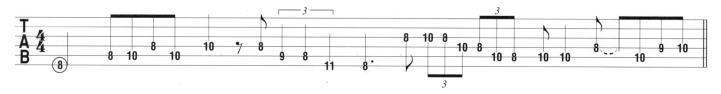

CHORD NAMES

Draw a line to match each chord on the left with its correct name on the right.

     E7

     A7

     F

     D7

     G7

     Cadd9

     C7

     B7

SYMBOLS & TERMS

Draw a line to match each symbol on the left with its correct name on the right.

     Coda Sign

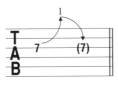   Whole Step

     Shuffle Feel

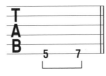   Bend and Release

   B♭ Major Scale

     Half Step

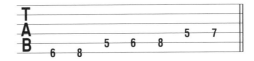   Vibrato

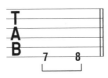   B Minor Pentatonic Scale

Write the note names in the spaces provided.

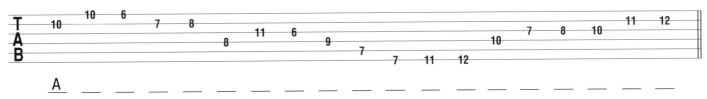

A _ _ _ _ _ _ _ _ _ _ _ _ _ _

Add bar lines.

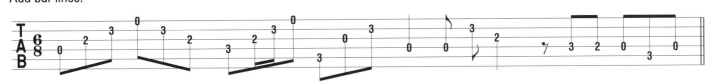

WARM-UP EXERCISES

Practice the following patterns and drills with a metronome. Start slowly and gradually build speed.

1-2-3-4

Play this pattern up and down the guitar neck using alternate picking.

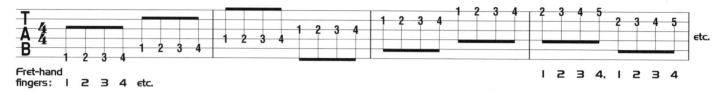

Fret-hand fingers: 1 2 3 4 etc.

1-3-2-4

Here's a variation of the first exercise. Try it starting with a downstroke; then try starting with an upstoke.

4-2-3-1

This variation starts with the pinky finger. Try experimenting with other variations on your own.

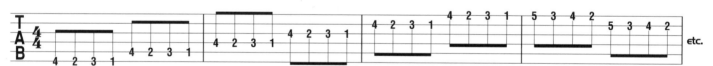

THE SPIDER

This exercise weaves it way from string to string. Be sure to maintain strict alternate picking while keeping an even tempo.

Fret-hand fingers: 1 2 3 4, 1 2 3 4 etc.

THE BUMBLEBEE

Try picking with just the tip of the pick to reduce travel time between strokes. Repeat many times.

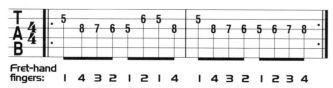

Fret-hand fingers: 1 4 3 2 1 2 1 4   1 4 3 2 1 2 3 4

THE WORM

Now's let's cross strings and frets. Keep your hands relaxed and enjoy the eerie sounds.

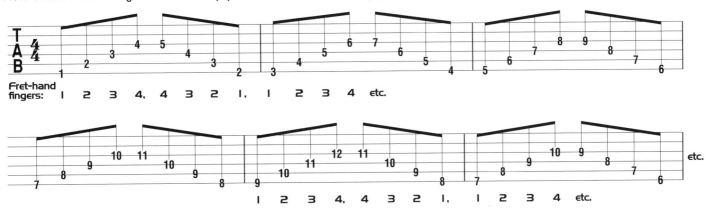

THE GRASSHOPPER

Here's a common pattern derived from the major scale that ascends and descends in thirds.

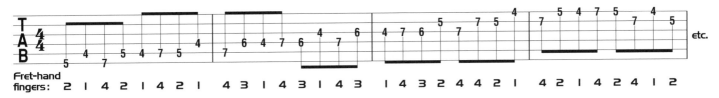

THE STAIRCASE

This exercise is also based on the major scale. It steps up and down in a pattern of fours. First play it in the key of A as written, and then try it in other keys.

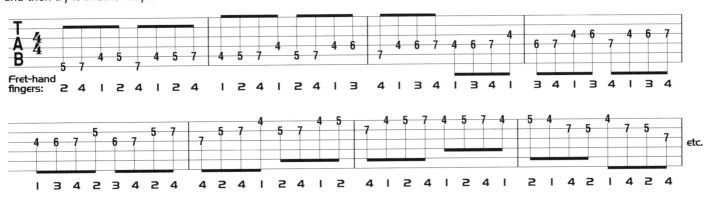

THE BUTTERFLY

Use continuous pull-offs and hammer-ons to execute this slippery legato lick. Do your best to sound each note at an even volume, and keep your rhythm steady.

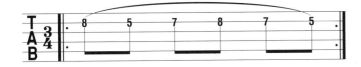

THE TRILL

Rapidly alternate between the notes using hammer-ons and pull-offs. Use different finger combinations. For example, try using your 3rd (ring) and 4th (pinky) fingers, which are usually not as strong or coordinated as other pairs.

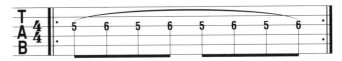

RELATIVE TUNING

Here are two methods for getting your guitar in tune when no other pitch source is available. To tune the guitar "to itself," we'll leave the 6th string as is and tune the other strings *relative* to it.

THE 5th-FRET PROCESS

1. Press the 6th string at the 5th fret. This is A. Tune the open 5th string to this pitch. To do this, let both notes ring together. If they don't quite match, determine whether the 5th string is higher or lower than the fretted 6th string note, and adjust the 5th string's tuning key accordingly.

2. Press the 5th string at the 5th fret. This is D. Tune the open 4th string to this pitch. Compare and adjust the 4th string as described in #1.

3. Press the 4th string at the 5th fret. This is G. Tune the open 3rd string to this pitch. Compare and adjust the 3rd string.

4. Press the 3rd string at the 4th fret. This is B. Tune the open 2nd string to this pitch. Compare and adjust the 2nd string.

5. Press the 2nd string at the 5th fret. This is E. Tune the open 1st string to this pitch. Compare and adjust the 1st string.

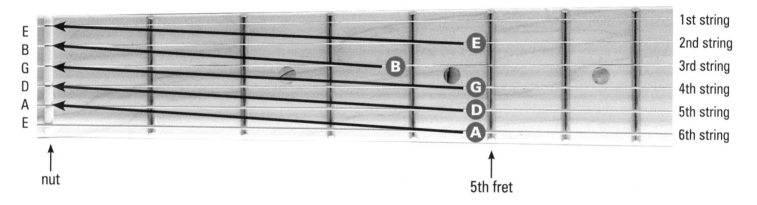

TUNING WITH HARMONICS

This process is similar to the 5th-fret process above, but uses natural harmonics rather than fretted notes. Some guitarists prefer this method because the notes continue ringing without fretting, thereby freeing your hand to adjust the tuning key. The sound "waves" can also be easier to hear from the chiming, harmonic tones.

1. Lightly touch the 6th string directly above the 5th fret wire, and pick the string to produce a harmonic. Let that note ring while you play the harmonic at the 7th fret of the 5th string. When the pitches are far apart, the "waves" of the two ringing harmonics will produce a fast oscillation. As you adjust the higher of the two strings, the waves will become slower the closer the string comes to the correct pitch. When the waves disappear, the string is in tune. Determine whether the 5th string is higher or lower than the 6th string, and adjust the 5th string's tuning key accordingly.

2. Play the harmonic on the 5th string, 5th fret and compare it with the harmonic on the 4th string, 7th fret.

3. Play the harmonic on the 4th string, 5th fret and compare it with the harmonic on the 3rd string, 7th fret.

4. Play the harmonic on the 3rd string, 4th fret and compare it with the harmonic on the 2nd string, 5th fret.

5. Play the harmonic on the 2nd string, 5th fret and compare it with the harmonic on the 1st string, 7th fret.

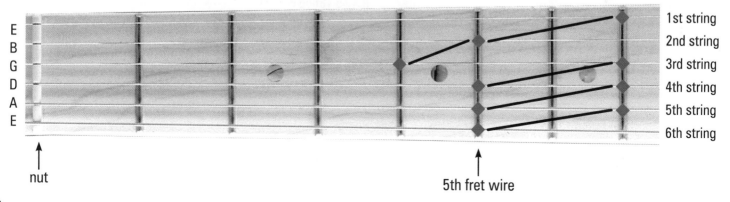

GEAR

Here are some basic guidelines to consider when choosing the right equipment for your desired sound and style.

ACOUSTIC GUITARS

There are two types of acoustic guitars: steel string and nylon string. The **steel-string** acoustic is generally played with a pick or fingerpicked. The strings have a bright tone, with plenty of volume when picked hard. The **nylon string** is also called a classical guitar. This instrument is typically picked with the fingers, and has a mellow tone that is quieter than a steel-string guitar.

The most important element when selecting an acoustic guitar is its size. You'll want the body of the guitar to fit you comfortably, with a neck that can easily be fretted. Nylon-string guitars typically have a smaller body than most steel-string models, but a much wider neck. Due to the internal construction of the instruments, you do not want to put nylon strings on a steel-string guitar, or vice versa.

The types of wood that the instruments are made of also dramatically affect the tone. Spruce is the species most commonly used for the top, although mahogany, cedar, and even man-made materials like carbon fiber have been utilized. Instruments with solid tops will have the best sonic properties, but are susceptible to changes in temperature and humidity. Laminated tops are generally less expensive and the best choice if you want to play outdoors. Rosewood and mahogany are the most common species used for the back and sides, but koa and curly maple are also popular. Another feature on some acoustics is called a "cutaway," which improves access above the 12th fret. Various models also have a factory-installed pickup so the guitar can be amplified, although pickups can be retrofit on any guitar. Choose the guitar that fits your playing style and sounds best to your ears.

Steel-String   Nylon-String   Cutaway

ELECTRIC GUITARS

There are three general types of electric guitars: solidbody, hollowbody, and semi-hollowbody. The **solidbody guitar** is associated most with rock, blues, country, and soul. The most popular models include the Fender Stratocaster, Gibson Les Paul, Paul Reed Smith, Fender Telecaster, Gibson SG, and the Ibanez RG. The solidbody guitar is typically heavier than others. Its density permits more sustain and makes it better suited for high-volume playing. The **hollowbody guitar** is the choice of most jazz guitarists. It is distinguished by its arched top and back, f-shaped sound holes, and deep sides. The most popular models include the Gibson ES-175, Gibson L-5, Gibson Super 400, Epiphone Emperor, Heritage Eagle, Guild Manhattan, and various models by D'Angelico, D'Aquisto, and Benedetto. The tone of the hollowbody guitar is more subdued than that of the solidbody, and its basic design makes it better suited for low to mid volume playing. The **semi-hollowbody guitar** has a thin, semi-hollow body with a solid wooden strip in the center. The most popular models include the Gibson ES-355, Gibson ES-345, Guild Starfire IV, Heritage H-535, and the Epiphone Sheraton. It is most commonly used by blues, jazz-rock, and rock guitarists, and is known for providing the best of both worlds in terms of tone: more crisp than a hollowbody and more mellow than a solidbody.

Pickups are the next sonic element to consider when buying a new electric guitar or choosing a replacement on an existing guitar. There are two general types of pickups: humbucking (double-coil) and single-coil. **Humbucking pickups** produce a dark, mellow sound when playing with a clean tone and a thick, heavy sound when playing with a distorted tone. **Single-coil pickups** produce a glassy, percussive sound when playing with a clean tone and an aggressive, biting sound when playing with a distorted tone.

The playability of various guitars is subjective. In trying to decide on a prospective guitar, consider the neck radius, scale length, neck material (rosewood, maple, ebony), string gauge, and fret size.

Fender Stratocaster

Gibson ES-175 Hollowbody

Gibson ES-335 Semi-Hollowbody

AMPS

There are two general types of amps: tube and solid-state. **Tube amps** are so-named because they are powered by and get their tonal characteristics from vacuum tubes. They produce a warm, smooth, clean tone and, when the volume is turned up, a natural distortion. They are favored by most blues, jazz, country, and roots-rock guitarists. **Solid-state amps** use transistors for power and tone. They are typically more reliable and versatile than tube amps and have come a long way in recent years in terms of being able to produce a warm tone. In the late 1990s, digital modeling technology has enabled solid-state amps to access an assortment of classic tube amp tones and a myriad of effects. Solid-state amps are preferred by most modern rock guitarists, but are also widely used for playing all musical styles.

| Vox AC30 Tube Amp | Peavey Half-stack | Line 6 Spider IV Modeling Amp |

EFFECTS

Effects are devices that plug in between your guitar and amp and enable you to alter your signal in a variety of ways. They are available as individual units called **foot pedals**, or as an all-in-one box, called a **multi-effects processor**. Following is a list of the most popular effects:

Distortion	Simulates the sound of a guitar signal driven too hard for the amp; the effect can produce anything from a bright, fuzzy tone to a thick, dirty tone.
Chorus	Simulates the sound of two guitars playing at once; the effect can produce anything from a lush, chiming sound to a warbled, fluttering sound.
Delay or Echo	Simulates the repetition of sound; the effect can add depth to your tone by producing anything from a short, "slap-back" delay to a longer, ambient looping sound.
Wah-Wah Pedal	Produces a sweeping, vocal-like tone by rocking the treadle back and forth.

PICKS

The key elements to consider when selecting picks are size, shape, material, texture, and gauge. Select a pick that's easy to grasp. Most are made of various plastics (celluloid, nylon), while some are made of more dense materials such as stone or metal. Generally, a thin gauge pick will work better for strumming, while a thicker pick will give a more aggressive attack for soloing. The material used also affects the tone (bright or dark) and the durability. Picks are the least expensive way to dramatically change your tone. Buy an assortment and have fun experimenting.

CHANGING STRINGS

If you break a string, or your strings sound dull and lifeless, you'll need to know how to change them. The methods for restringing vary from guitar to guitar, so follow the directions that correspond with your instrument.

REMOVING STRINGS

To remove an old string, simply turn the tuning peg to loosen the string, and then remove it from the tuner and bridge. Bridge pins on acoustic guitars sometimes stick, so you may need to use a tool to carefully pry them out. You can replace strings one at a time for tuning convenience, or remove all six before restringing.

ELECTRIC GUITARS

Here are the steps for restringing electric guitars.

1. Insert the string through the hole at the bridge until the ball end catches. On Fender-type guitars, this is done through the back plate (Photo A); on Gibson-types, it's done on the back side of the bridge (Photo B)

Photo A

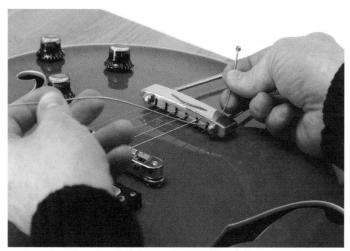

Photo B

2. Run the string through the posthole of the tuner. Allow a couple inches of slack between the tuner and the bridge so there's enough string to wind around the post three or four times. While holding the slack string, bend the tail of the string above the posthole at a 90-degree angle (Photo C). For Fender-style guitars with six tuners in a row, all of the strings will wind counterclockwise. For Gibson-type guitars, the high three strings will wind clockwise and the low three strings will wind counterclockwise (Diagram A).

3. Use one hand to keep the string tight against the nut, and your other hand to turn the tuning peg until the string is up to pitch (Photo D). Make sure the string is nested in the proper grooves in the nut and bridge before tightening fully. Cut off any excess string above the tuning peg when you're finished.

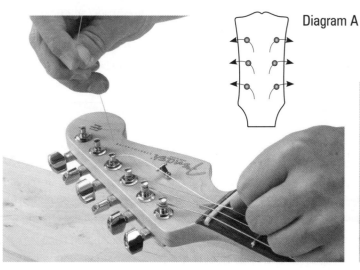

Diagram A

Photo C

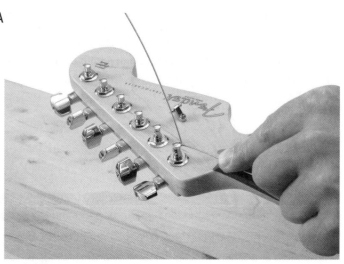

Photo D

ACOUSTIC GUITARS

Here are the steps for restringing a steel-string acoustic guitar.

1. Insert the ball end of the string into the bridge hole that held the bridge pin.

2. Wedge the bridge pin back in the hole with the slot facing forward, toward the fretboard (Photos E and F). Do not firmly lodge the pin in place yet.

Photo E

Photo F

3. Pull the string back gently until it rests against the underside of the pin. Then firmly lodge the pin in place.

4. Run the string through the posthole of the tuner. Allow a couple inches of slack between the tuner and the bridge so there is enough string to wind around the post three or four times. While holding the slack string, bend the tail of the string above the posthole at a 90-degree angle. The high three strings will wind clockwise around the post, while the low three strings will wind counterclockwise (see Diagram A on previous page).

5. Use one hand to keep the string tight against the nut, and your other hand to turn the tuning peg until the string is up to pitch (see Photo D on previous page). Make sure the string is nested in the proper grooves in the nut before tightening fully. Cut off any excess string above the tuning peg when you're finished.

STRINGING TIP

New strings need to be "stretched out" before you can expect them to hold their pitch. You can do this by pulling on each string one at a time with your fingers (over the pickups or soundhole, away from your body) after you've strung up your guitar, then retuning each of them to the correct pitch. Repeat this until each string stays in tune even after you've pulled on it.

Rhythm Tab Legend

Rhythm Tab is a form of notation that adds rhythmic values to the traditional tab staff.

TABLATURE graphically represents the guitar fingerboard. Each horizontal line represents a string, and each number represents a fret. Rhythmic values are shown using ovals, stems, and dots.

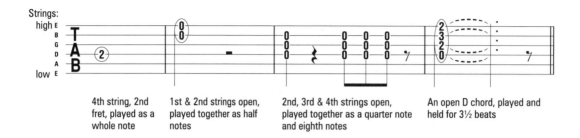

| 4th string, 2nd fret, played as a whole note | 1st & 2nd strings open, played together as half notes | 2nd, 3rd & 4th strings open, played together as a quarter note and eighth notes | An open D chord, played and held for 3½ beats |

Definitions for Special Guitar Notation

HALF-STEP BEND: Strike the note and bend up 1/2 step.

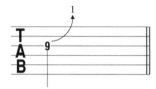

WHOLE-STEP BEND: Strike the note and bend up one step.

QUARTER-STEP BEND: Strike the note and bend up 1/4 step.

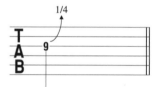

BEND AND RELEASE: Strike the note and bend up as indicated, then release back to the original note. Only the first note is struck.

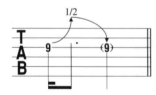

PRE-BEND: Bend the note as indicated, then strike it.

VIBRATO: The string is vibrated by rapidly bending and releasing the note with the fretting hand.

HAMMER-ON: Strike the first (lower) note with one finger, then sound the higher note (on the same string) with another finger by fretting it without picking.

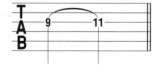

PULL-OFF: Place both fingers on the notes to be sounded. Strike the first note, and without picking, pull the finger off to sound the second (lower) note.

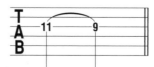

LEGATO SLIDE: Strike the first note and then slide the same fret-hand finger up or down to the second note. The second note is not struck.

SHIFT SLIDE: Same as legato slide, except the second note is struck.

GRACE-NOTE SLUR: Strike the note and immediately hammer-on (pull-off or slide) as indicated.

TRILL: Very rapidly alternate between the notes indicated by continuously hammering on and pulling off.

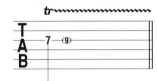

NATURAL HARMONIC: Strike the note while the fret hand lightly touches the string directly over the fret indicated.

Harm.

MUFFLED STRINGS: A percussive sound is produced by laying the fret hand across the string(s) without depressing, and striking them with the pick hand.

PALM MUTING: The note is partially muted by the pick hand lightly touching the string(s) just before the bridge.

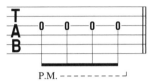

P.M. - - - - - - - - -

Additional Musical Definitions

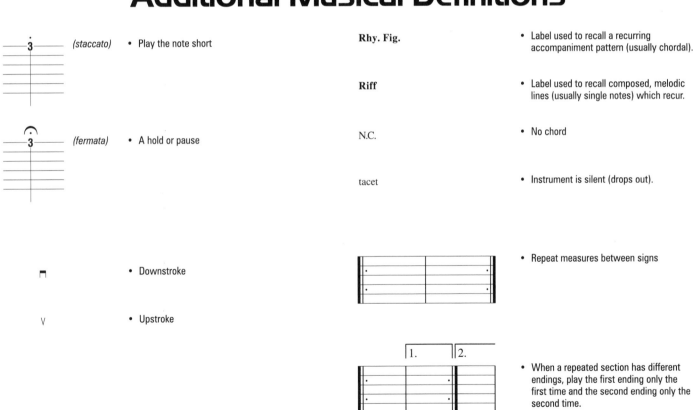

(staccato)	• Play the note short	
(fermata)	• A hold or pause	
	• Downstroke	
	• Upstroke	
D.S. al Coda	• Go back to the sign (𝄋), then play until the measure marked *"To Coda,"* then skip to the section labelled *"Coda."*	
D.C. al Fine	• Go back to the beginning of the song and play until the measure marked *"Fine"* (end).	

Rhy. Fig. • Label used to recall a recurring accompaniment pattern (usually chordal).

Riff • Label used to recall composed, melodic lines (usually single notes) which recur.

N.C. • No chord

tacet • Instrument is silent (drops out).

• Repeat measures between signs

• When a repeated section has different endings, play the first ending only the first time and the second ending only the second time.

• Repeat previous measure

• Repeat previous two measures

NOTE: Tablature numbers in parentheses are used when:
- The note is sustained, but a new articulation begins (such as a hammer-on, pull-off, slide, or bend), or
- A bend is released.